I'll Never Marry A Farmer

Lois Hole

ON LIFE, LEARNING & VEGETABLE GARDENING

Photography by
Akemi Matsubuchi

HOLE'S

PUBLISHED BY HOLE'S
101 Bellerose Drive
St. Albert, Alberta, Canada
T8N 8N8

Printed in Canada   5   4   3   2   1

I'll Never Marry a Farmer
Copyright © 1998 Lois Hole

ISBN 0-9682791-1-2 (standard hardcover)
ISBN 0-9682791-2-0 (deluxe hardcover)

Canadian Cataloguing in Publication Data

Hole, Lois, 1933–
  I'll never marry a farmer

ISBN 0-9682791-1-2

  1. Hole, Lois, 1933- 2. Gardeners—Prairie Provinces—Biography. 3. Vegetable gardening—Prairie Provinces. I. Title.
SB63.H64A3 1998   635'.092   C98-910836-8

Prepress by Elite Lithographers, Edmonton, Alberta
Printed and bound by Friesens, Altona, Manitoba
∞ Printed on acid-free paper

Contents

Acknowledgements

We wish to thank the following people for their assistance:

Coralee and Adrienne Farrell; Joan Green; Nell and
Jack Greening; Joel and Eric Grice; the Harris family;
Jack Hughes; Kathryn and Michael Hole; Zachary Keith;
Kuhlmann's Market Gardens and Greenhouses;
Karen Marshall; Hisaye Matsubuchi; Donna Powell;
Emily and Anne Rogers; the *St. Albert Gazette*;
Bob Todrick; Ralph Vandenberg, Vandenberg's Jewellers;
Eddie and Cecile Vion; Vicky Zou; and especially all the
staff here at Hole's for their time, energy, and ideas.

For Ted, who helped me to discover my talents and who encouraged me to share my strengths.

—and—

For farm-women everywhere, who will understand. You have taught me so much and I'm proud to be one of you.

Preface

On Life, Learning, & Vegetable Gardening

ON LIFE...people, places, and events that have shaped who I am. Sometimes funny, sometimes sad, these experiences have affected me deeply. Meet my family, friends, and staff, and discover the gifts each person has shared with me.

ON LEARNING...lessons I've drawn from my experiences and observations. Every day holds challenges and opportunities for us, from which we can learn and grow if we choose. Learning occurs at the oddest moments, and we are always enriched by it.

ON VEGETABLE GARDENING...secrets of my vegetable patch. Each chapter contains personal recollections and advice on an assortment of vegetables. I've included tips that have helped us get more from our garden, plus practical suggestions that may help you get more from yours.

So many of you have invited me to share my thoughts with you, and in return have shared yours with me. I hope this volume allows you a glimpse of the wonder and delight I have had from my garden. ❧

Introduction
Blind Luck

SOMETIMES, WHEN I THINK about where I am today, I feel like I'm a million miles away from my childhood. Our lives can take so many crazy, unpredictable twists and turns that it almost seems as if we're ruled by chance.

Luck has certainly played a role in my life's journey. Yet in many ways, we make our own luck, by recognizing the right paths when we come to them. Looking at it that way, my real luck began with my parents. The outlook and ideals they instilled in me have helped me to make good choices throughout my life. For instance, when chance sent a young fellow named Ted Hole my way, I was able to sense that he was the man for me.

Growing up in the tiny town of Buchanan, Saskatchewan, I often imagined the kind of man I would marry. Like any young girl, I continually changed my image of the perfect man, depending on how old I was or what movie I had seen that week. However, I knew exactly what I *didn't* want in a husband. I always told my mother, "No matter what, I'll never marry a farmer."

To me, farms seemed like the loneliest places on earth. I much preferred the feeling of being surrounded by people and activity, even though Buchanan wasn't exactly a bustling metropolis. Once, when a friend's mother convinced me to come for a holiday at their farm, I ended up crying myself to sleep for four nights straight. I wasn't invited back.

No, the husband of my dreams was definitely not wearing bib overalls. But then I met Ted.

In 1950, Ted was in the middle of his Bachelor of Agriculture program at the University of Alberta in Edmonton. I was involved with a person that my mother called "a good prospect," a dashing, responsible young man who had a managerial position with Trans Canada Airlines. As far as my mother was concerned, I had it made. I was pretty happy with my young man, too. My future seemed set.

But fate intervened. My friend Sheila, a nurse, happened to be friends with Ted and had promised to be his date for a Faculty of Agriculture dance later that week. But she got called in to work at the last minute and couldn't attend.

She didn't want to leave Ted without a date, so she offered to set him up with one of her friends. Before Sheila could open her mouth to make a suggestion, Ted said, "Sure. How about that blonde one...Lois?" Ted had seen me a couple of times in passing, although I have to admit that I hadn't noticed him at all.

Sheila had been about to name another friend but couldn't see any graceful way to refuse Ted's suggestion. "All right," she replied, "I'll ask her." And so I received a phone call shortly afterward.

"Well, sure I'll go," I said agreeably.

Those simple words sealed my fate. Ted turned out to be a pretty handsome guy—I thought he looked like Charlton Heston. I could tell right away how sincere and honest he was.

After a few more dates, he told me that he wanted to farm as soon as he graduated, that even though he had a trade as a plumber, he felt a deep connection to the earth, that he couldn't imagine a better life than on a farm. He spoke with such passion that I found myself being caught up in the romantic notion of marrying a handsome farmer—despite my childhood vow.

Ted brought me out to the property he had in mind, a small patch of land on the banks of the Sturgeon River. Because the farm was so close to Edmonton, my childhood fears of isolation were crowded out by other, much happier memories.

As a girl, I spent countless hours helping my mother in the garden. Though I didn't always realize it, they were some of the happiest times in my childhood. For my mother, gardening was more of a pleasure than a chore, and she instilled the same feeling in me. If I helped her weed the carrots or water the tomatoes, it wasn't because she made me do it. I did it because I wanted to. As I looked at Ted, it suddenly seemed to make sense for me to build my future life around growing things.

My mother also gave me a love of music. She was the organist in our local church and played the piano at home almost every day. On days when I was less than enthusiastic about helping in the garden, she'd say to me, "Why don't you go on inside and practise the piano?" As a teenager, I became the church's substitute organist, and eventually I earned a diploma from the Toronto Conservatory. Ted wasn't a classical musician, but he loved to play the saxophone—and sometimes even got paid for it! If I ended up with him, I knew there would always be plenty of music in my life.

I also thought of my father. He was a strongly principled man, with deeply held convictions. He raised me to look at life with clear eyes: to judge for myself what was right and what was wrong and to act accordingly. He also showed me, through his example, the value of good, hard work. Standing next to Ted, I sensed the same kind of strength in him.

A few days later, I faced the awkward task of breaking up with my Trans Canada boyfriend. Mom was not amused.

"Lois, Ted seems like a nice boy, but *really*, didn't you always tell me you would never marry a farmer?"

"Well, yes, Mom, but…."

"You always said that farms were the loneliest places you knew."

"I know, but…."

It went on that way for a while. Ted was hard to resist, though, and he won Mom over soon enough. Dad was even easier to convince: he'd always backed me in whatever (or whomever) I chose to pursue. "Marry the one you love, Lois, whoever that happens to be."

Ted's father, on the other hand, presented more of a challenge. Mr. Hole was an impressive figure, and I trembled a little the day he invited Ted and me home for a "chat" about our future plans.

"How are you going to handle farm life, Lois? You know it's not easy. How are you going to help make ends meet? Are you prepared for a lot of backbreaking work?" The questions came thick and fast. Mr. Hole paused only occasionally to take a puff from his pipe.

To this day, I wonder whether he simply didn't think a city girl was up to the challenge or whether he was trying, in his own gruff way, to warn me about the hardships that might lie ahead. Was he remarkably insightful about the important role that women play on the farm or simply chauvinistic? Still, I found it ironic that

I was getting grilled, even though Ted was the one who wanted to pursue this whole notion of farming.

It was quite an ordeal, but I kept my composure and answered honestly, determined to prove that I was "right for the job." At the end of the interview, Ted's father seemed reasonably satisfied. Ted and I breathed a sigh of relief. With parental barriers hurdled, all that remained was the wedding.

When the big event arrived, it was the happiest day of my life. Everything went exactly according to plan—until after the service.

Rather than a car, Ted and I were to drive off in a horse-drawn carriage. We were sitting at the back of the cart on a couple of bales of hay when something startled the horses, causing them to leap forward suddenly. I lost my balance and felt myself tipping over backwards, my feet flying into the air. Several people gasped, sure I was going to crack my head open on the pavement.

But like a knight in shining armour, Ted came to my rescue. He scooped me up in one arm and kissed me, as everyone applauded and cheered.

After the wedding, Ted's mother came up to me and said, "Lois, you're very lucky to have married my son." I could only smile and nod. "You're right...Mother."

Thanks to luck and good judgement, not only did I marry a farmer, I became one.

৯৯৯

And together, Ted and I have been growing great things ever since.

Location

"Location is everything" might be a real estate catch-phrase, but I'll bet it was a gardener who said it first. You always have to find just the right place for your plants. Each year you try something a bit different. You suffer through your failures, celebrate your successes, and hopefully learn something from each one.

After watching your tender, sensitive cucumbers wither in the breeze for a few years, you decide to nestle them in the most protected corner of your garden. Then you plant a few hills of corn nearby, to give those cucumbers some tall, husky bodyguards. After finding out the hard way that peas and spinach like it cool, you find them a spot away from the scorching midday sun (save that for the peppers and tomatoes!). Above all, you learn to put the lettuce as close as possible to the kitchen door, so you can dash out and pick a salad just before suppertime!

When my husband Ted and I first arrived on our farm just north of St. Albert, Alberta, we hadn't the first idea what we were going to do with it. Ted had just completed his degree in agriculture, but that didn't exactly make us farmers. As a child, I had spent only brief periods on my grandparents' farm, and Ted couldn't claim even that much experience.

Still, the day we stood together for the first time on that gently sloping hillside, gazing down toward the Sturgeon River, we knew we had found the right place. We were young and we had a gorgeous piece of land: our potential seemed limitless.

Ted reached down and grabbed a handful of topsoil, squeezed it in his fist, and smelled it. I was surprised that somebody who hadn't been brought up on a farm would ever think to do that. There's a beautiful smell to good soil, particularly when it's a little damp. Ted, from his courses at university, knew that. He inhaled deeply, then turned to me and said, "This is number one soil." It was so black, so deep, so rich, and so wonderful. He knew we could grow practically anything we wanted on this land.

Of course, no matter how perfect your little corner of earth, finding the right use for it takes a certain amount of trial and error. And in those first years, we certainly had our share of trials and errors. We tried grain, but at 200 acres, our farm wasn't nearly big enough for that. We tried chickens and found we didn't have the right facilities. We tried pigs, we tried turkeys, we tried cattle—nothing seemed to work out.

During those lean times, we developed a few tricks to get by. I'd say to Ted, "Let's go to my mom's for supper tonight." And then we'd go to his mother's for supper the next night. I have to admit it was a conscious strategy on our part. Of course, the benefits reached far beyond the money we saved on groceries. Parents always love to see their kids, and those frequent visits brought us that much closer together. But parents can offer only so much shelter. In the end, we still had to fend for ourselves. Sometimes, our lack of experience was positively comical—although I must admit it didn't always seem so at the time.

One winter, we were really struggling to make ends meet. Ted was working in Edmonton to pay off the debts from our previous year's mishaps (this was a recurring pattern in those days). I stayed at home and tended the cattle.

One of my jobs was to keep their trough filled with water. Well, it was one of the coldest winters you could imagine, just desperately cold, and our pump kept

freezing up. Every evening we'd be out in the barn, thawing out the darned pump. One time we even had a friend come out with a blowtorch. No matter what we tried, by morning Ted was off to work and I was left at home with a frozen pump. I finally resorted to melting snow, working all day just trying to keep the cattle in water.

Much later, long after the weather had warmed up, Ted told our tale of woe to a farmer friend. He came over to our place, took one look at the pump, and said, "You know, the problem is that your pump doesn't have a drain hole." All we needed was one tiny hole to allow the water to drain back down and that pump would never have frozen. It was that simple.

The funniest part was we never got discouraged. I still wonder about that. I guess I always had the feeling that since it couldn't get any worse, it would have to get better. We had found our place in the world, and by God we were going to make it work.

Eventually, of course, I was proven right. It took us quite a few years, but we finally figured out how to make the most of our location. Even through the hardest years, while we struggled with our wheat, chickens, and cattle, our vegetable garden kept thriving. When people started stopping by the side of the road, offering money for our extra produce, the light bulb finally came on.

To this day, our vegetable garden sits right next to our old house, on the very patch of land where Ted first smelled the soil. Trees protect it on three sides, and its gentle southward slope seems custom-made to catch the spring sunshine. Every year we're able to get onto the land weeks ahead of most of our neighbours, and we enjoy some of the earliest and most bountiful crops you could imagine.

Like the plants in a garden, people will flourish if they find the right location. After more than 40 years on our farm—years of frustration and triumph, of sorrow and joy, of hard, dirty work and good, clean fun—I can't imagine living anywhere else.

...constant love and attention...

Cucumbers

IT DIDN'T TAKE US LONG to figure out that cucumbers are like babies: they need constant love and attention to grow up happy. These delicate plants do best in a safe, cozy place, and they need heat!—if the soil could stay moist and warm all season long, they'd love it. If you grow corn, try planting cucumbers close by: corn acts as a windbreak and traps heat. Make sure the corn isn't *too* close, though—you don't want cornstalks shading your cucumbers. Another good spot for cucumbers to settle is next to a fence: fences provide shelter and a place to climb.

The most challenging part of growing cucumbers is getting the darn seeds to germinate—they need a lot of heat right from the start. Over the years, we've tried several methods to ensure a large crop. We've put hot caps over every plant, mixed seed into peat moss before planting, used black plastic to cover the fields for weed suppression and soil warming—even tried covering the plants with "tunnels" (essentially mini-greenhouses). These methods proved too labour-intensive, though, and in the end, we returned to seeding heavily in a number of different locations. By planting cucumbers this way, we can be sure that at least some of them will grow. If you succeed in growing a big batch of cucumbers, you should be very proud, for these are among the most difficult vegetables to bring to fruition.

Pollination is vital

Our neighbours, the Sernowskis, had beehives fairly close to our cucumber patch. When there were a lot of bees, we could count on a large crop of cucumbers, thanks to the bees' efforts in pollinating. The bees made such a difference that we eventually set up our own beehives near our cucumber field.

In the field

When working with cucumbers, I'm always careful not to splash water and mud on the foliage. That's because doing so can spread soil-borne diseases, to which cucumbers are very vulnerable. The plants can deteriorate quickly under these conditions. Never work in the cucumber patch when it's wet.

Avoid picking cucumbers before noon—wait until all the dew has evaporated and the vines are no longer brittle. This way you can harvest the ripe cucumbers without damaging the plant.

- During hot, sunny weather, I've seen cucumber vines grow several inches in a single day!
- Cucumbers were once considered poisonous, perhaps because of their tough, bitter rind. We now know that cucumbers are a good source of iron and vitamins.

Cuke of Choice: Cool Breeze

I just love this cucumber—it's so well-named! It's crisp and juicy, like biting into a bit of springtime, and it's not at all bitter. It's also produces fruit without pollination, eliminating the need to plant both male and female plants.

Cucumbers are frost-sensitive, so I don't seed most of them until late May or early June; but I still gamble with a few. Most varieties will give you 10 cucumbers per plant, but many hybrids produce twice as many.

Accidental Gardening

SOMETIMES A LOCATION will work out for you in ways you never imagined. My garden happened to be right next to a well-travelled road, and that seemingly insignificant detail changed our lives forever.

Farm women everywhere tend to get carried away when they plant their gardens. By mid-July we're half buried in produce. You can't give the stuff away. My friend Roger Swain, host of *The Victory Garden* on PBS, jokes that, come harvest time in his Massachusetts hometown, you always leave your car doors locked and the windows rolled up. Otherwise, when you come back, you'll find the car filled with zucchini.

One sunny morning, I had just come back from picking the year's very first pail of cucumbers. I was about to go out and pick more, because there were so many of them. It had been a glorious spring and early summer.

Just then, a car pulled into the yard and two men got out. They had been driving by and spotted my huge, thriving garden. They didn't speak much English, but they managed to ask if I would sell them some fresh cucumbers.

So I brought out my pail, and they looked at the cucumbers I had just picked. They were the firmest, most beautiful cucumbers you ever saw in your life. The fellows tried their best to look nonchalant, in order to get a good price. I could tell by the gleam in their eyes, however, that I could charge them just about anything I wanted.

Still, when they asked me "How much?", I had no idea what to answer. I had never sold vegetables before. We didn't even have a scale. I looked at this big five-gallon pail of cucumbers and tried to decide how much it weighed. I said, "I really don't know how many pounds this might be." One of the men frowned and said, "Ooooh, I'd say maybe six or seven pounds." Of course, I knew they were kidding me. There had to be a good 25 or 30 pounds in there.

So I said to them, "I'll tell you what: I'll let you have the whole pail for two dollars." And that was when I learned my first lesson in marketing. I should have said three, because now they started to bargain with me. I ended up selling those cucumbers for a dollar!

Of course, about a week later, those fellows were back for more. As soon as they got out of their car, I told them, "This time it's going to cost you more than a dollar."

But those two fellows started it all. Ted and I figured that if they were so interested in our vegetables, maybe other people would be too. We put a tiny ad in the *Edmonton Journal*. It cost us $2.50 for one full week. All the ad said was "Hole's Farm—Vegetables for Sale," and our phone number. Well, our phone just rang off the hook.

Before long, we were dealing with twenty or so customers every day. At that time, Edmonton had a lot of recent Italian immigrants, and they were just dying for home-grown garden produce. People would phone us up, and we would tell them what we had that day.

We were lucky that it had been such a good growing year. Our production was about twice what it would be in an ordinary summer. Even so, we couldn't come close to keeping up with the demand.

One evening, after the last car had pulled out of our yard, I counted up the day's receipts: 36 dollars! The total was staggering. I just couldn't believe it. "Ted," I said delightedly, "we've struck gold!"

The die was cast. After years of trial and error, of trying to find the perfect use for our land, we finally had our answer.

When you stop and think about it, if I hadn't planted my garden next to the road, where those two fellows could see it as they drove by, we might never have gone into the gardening business. I guess if you're in the right location at the right time, wonderful accidents have a way of happening! ❧

The Old Red Barn

WHEN TED FIRST SUGGESTED we move our vegetable business into the old barn, I was dead set against the idea.

I had nothing against the building, mind you. A well-loved local landmark, it had stood prominently alongside the road for decades. When people spotted it, they knew they were almost in town. Or if they were driving the other way, the sight of the barn told them that they were truly out in the country.

I preferred looking at the barn from the outside. I loved selling vegetables and eggs in the open air. We had our tables set out under the trees, and I couldn't think of a nicer place to spend the day. I wasn't keen to swap all that fresh air and sunshine for the gloomy, musty interior of a barn.

But I could certainly see Ted's point. On hot summer days, we'd be up bright and early picking crisp, gorgeous lettuce, and by noon it would look as if it had spent the better part of a week on a truck. We'd see skeptical customers poking at the wilting, woebegone carrot tops and assure them, "We dug those just this morning." Wet days were even worse. We'd just stand there and watch the cars pass us by, their windows rolled up tightly against the rain.

Still, I needed some highly unusual persuasion before I agreed to make the move.

For some time, we had noticed that our cartons of eggs were occasionally one or two short. Ted even joked that I was having trouble counting to twelve.

One morning, walking across the lawn, I caught a glimpse of white out of the corner of my eye. There, nestled in the grass at my feet, was one of our missing eggs. Before long, we were all finding eggs. Ted spotted one in the garden, tucked among the cucumbers. The boys discovered one smashed on the driveway. One customer jokingly asked how we trained our chickens to lay eggs in the flowerbeds.

My son Bill finally solved the mystery. He noticed a large magpie flying rather unsteadily across the yard one day. As the bird wobbled closer, Bill could see an egg clutched in its claws. Suddenly, the feathered shoplifter dropped its cargo, then swooped down to see if the shell had broken. Finding the egg unscathed, the magpie flew away, disappointed.

Bill ran to tell us his discovery. When Ted finally stopped chuckling, he asked if now I'd be willing to move into the barn. Grudgingly, I gave my consent.

Of course, the task involved more than just relocating a few tables. For years the barn had served as our chicken coop. We kept the place reasonably tidy, but it was not fit for selling produce. Wisely, we decided to postpone the move until the following spring.

After weeks of shovelling, sweeping, scrubbing, and painting, the place was ready. Ted set it up beautifully, with rows of sloping tables and large baskets brimming with vegetables. We kept plenty of fresh shavings around, so it smelled heavenly.

We had a couple of lovely old scales with rolling dials. Since we never got around to having the things properly tested, I always gave people an extra pound here, a couple of pounds there, to make sure they were getting full value. People just loved that: it wasn't the sort of thing that happened in a big-city supermarket.

Best of all, even on the hottest afternoons, the barn was wonderfully cool and the vegetables stayed crisp and fresh. Customers drooping under the August heat perked up the moment they walked through the door. On Saturdays and Sundays, wives often lingered to chat. Their husbands spread blankets outside in the shade and lay there reading while the kids raced around the yard or climbed the trees. A simple shopping expedition turned into a real family outing.

In no time at all, that rustic old barn, with "Hole's Farm" freshly emblazoned on its side, became the cornerstone of our business. People loved it so much that we began featuring it in our ads: "Come out and get your vegetables at the old red barn." Our little local landmark was now famous for miles around, and we found ourselves selling more vegetables than we ever dreamed possible.

Today, even though the old red barn is long gone, it holds a big place in our hearts. It's no accident that our buildings are still a warm, rustic red.

And maybe that's why, unlike most farmers, I have a soft spot in my heart for magpies. ✆

Trial by Fire

WHEN WE WERE just starting out on our new farm, everything seemed extraordinarily precious to us. We often lost sleep over the health of our crops and livestock, fretting about how we would pay the bills if things went wrong.

That sort of feeling is natural, but you just can't get too caught up in material concerns. If you lose sight of what's really important, even for a few seconds, you can end up acting like an idiot.

Case in point: the day I ran into a flaming building to save a flock of turkeys.

We were raising about 200 of them that year, in a makeshift shed heated by a small wood stove. Ted was away working as a plumber in the city, leaving me alone to tend the farm during the day. I was pregnant at the time, as big as a house.

One morning, I happened to glance up through the kitchen window and saw flames shooting out of the turkey house. A pipe had overheated and ignited the wood around it. I raced across the yard and threw open the door to let the birds escape. But naturally, being turkeys, they just sat there.

So in I went, half blinded by the smoke, to shoo them out the door. Unfortunately, there was a second, smaller opening, built for the turkeys. You guessed it: as I chased them out the main door, they simply marched around the building and came back in the small door. I finally blocked the opening and managed to get almost all of the birds out. We ended up losing only about half a dozen.

Later, as I watched the flames devour the shed, the realization of what I had done began to set in. I had taken an absolutely terrifying risk. I could even picture the headline: "Pregnant woman dies rescuing turkeys." What a way to go.

It seems absurd now, but in the heat of the moment, I didn't even think twice. Those turkeys were our livelihood. What would we do if we lost them all?

The answer, of course, is easy. We would have picked up the pieces and moved on. It wouldn't have been the end of the world.

Except, that is, for the turkeys. ❧

Tomatoes on the 23rd Floor

GARDENS HAVE AN almost magical ability to transport us to another place, far away from our everyday stress and worries. Most people, even if they aren't gardeners, find it soothing to spend time among green, growing things.

You don't have to live on a farm to experience that magic. You can carve out a vegetable patch in a tiny urban back yard. You can fill a window box with potting soil and create a flowerbed on your apartment balcony. You can even tend tomatoes on the 23rd floor of an office tower.

That last example is a favourite story of mine. I think I first read it in the *Globe and Mail*. A corporate CEO, with a lavishly furnished corner office, vanished every day between the hours of twelve and one. His secretary held his calls and turned away all visitors. Meanwhile, the boss took off his jacket, rolled up his sleeves, and looked after his tomato plants. Every window was lined with them.

I love to think of him in there, placidly watering, fertilizing, and pruning, while the business world buzzed on around him. That was his time, and nothing could interfere with him and his tomatoes.

I'll bet those plants, treated to so much love, water, and sunlight, produced the best tomatoes ever seen on Bay Street.

During our market garden days, we often met folks like that CEO. Every so often, fancy cars would turn into the yard and men dressed in wing-tipped shoes and tailored suits would get out. They'd chat with us about the weather and carefully look over the fresh tomatoes, peas, corn, and beans. Some of them even went out to the field to pick their own.

I always thought that the vegetables were just a convenient excuse. What they really wanted—and needed—was to get out of their offices and onto the land, even for just a little while. It brought back something they'd lost, something from their childhood days. When they went up to that field on a sunny afternoon and looked out at that magnificent view, it gave them a wonderful feeling. At the same time, they could pick something nice for supper!

I remember finding a man up at the far end of the vegetable patch one afternoon, gazing out at our field of ripening wheat. He said, "You know, I grew up in Saskatchewan, but I had forgotten how beautiful a grain field looks."

That was the first time I saw him. After that, he was out in our field every single week. He didn't pick an awful lot, but I have the feeling he always came away well nourished. ❧

Branching Out

Even when you're firmly rooted in the perfect location, you still get the urge to branch out. Our farm has remained a focal point for both our family and our business, but that hasn't kept us from stretching our boundaries from time to time.

In our early market gardening years, we were forced to do quite a bit of branching out. Most people had no idea we were out in St. Albert growing vegetables. Since they weren't coming to us, we decided to go to them.

It was our second summer of growing vegetables, and we had an exceptionally early harvest. We had been able to work the soil in March and by mid-April had already done a lot of our seeding. The weather was perfect that year, and by late June we realized we were about to be up to our knees in vegetables.

So we took out an ad in the paper, sat back, and waited for the customers to start flooding in. And we waited. And we waited.

In those days, people didn't even think of market gardens in July. Because August and September were the traditional harvesting months, that's when folks expected to buy local produce.

With carrots and beets piling up around me, I realized the time had come for drastic action. I loaded the pickup with vegetables, piled the kids in the cab, and drove into Edmonton to sell our wares.

I pulled up to the Bel Air apartment complex, marched into a building, and knocked on the first door. A slightly startled housewife answered, and I asked her, "Would you like to buy some fresh garden vegetables?"

She followed me out to the truck. A minute or two later, a neighbour wandered out to see what was going on. Before I knew it, I was surrounded by women. As they bought up all my vegetables, they kept asking me, "When will you be back?"

For the next few weeks, I kept making return trips. By August, however, I had to give it up. My regular customers had finally begun to show up at the farm, and I couldn't be in two places at once. I felt bad about abandoning my new Bel Air friends, but fortunately, some of them managed to find me.

A few years later, we tried branching out again when a neighbour suggested we set up a stall at the City Market. Ted and I were far too busy, but we asked our boys, who were not quite ten and eleven years old, if they would like to tackle the project.

Bill and Jim knew it would be a lot of work. Still, they were proud that we would give them that kind of responsibility and independence—and the incentive of a little pocket money didn't hurt, either! Most importantly, the boys felt they were contributing to the family business.

Each Friday evening, they went out to the field to pick vegetables. Then at the crack of dawn, they dragged themselves out of bed to pick a few more. Ted helped them load the GM half-ton, then drove them to the market. By 7:30 a.m., the boys were set up and ready for business, and Ted headed back to the farm.

We weren't surprised when the boys, left on their own, learned a business lesson or two. Early one morning, Bill was thrilled when a customer walked up and offered to buy all the peas. The man asked for a discount, which seemed only fair considering the size of the purchase. He hauled the peas away, and Bill proudly counted the money. My son began to have misgivings, however, when he saw the man park the crates behind another stall down the row.

Sure enough, by noon every vendor in the market was fresh out of peas—except one. At that point, the man pulled out the crates, and proceeded to sell our peas at twice the price he had paid.

As the weeks went by, the boys' self-confidence grew. One customer asked Jim how much peas were, and Jim answered, forty cents a pound. "I'll give you twenty cents," the man said, walking off with a bag of peas. Jim, just ten years old, ran after him and grabbed those peas right out of his hand.

Bill and Jim also had to endure a fair bit of resentment from the other vendors—including some who had been very encouraging at first. Because the boys brought smaller batches of vegetables, picked as recently as possible, their produce was much fresher than anyone else's. In the eyes of their competitors, Bill and Jim were upsetting the "natural order."

It wasn't long before the boys grew tired of the brutal schedule and the rough-and-tumble atmosphere of the market. At the same time, Ted and I had come to realize just how much we relied on their help around the farm. For the good of our family, and the good of our business, we decided to once again focus all of our efforts at home.

In the process, though, Bill and Jim did a lot of growing up. They began to take a much more active and direct interest in the business and were always ready to voice an opinion—even when we didn't ask for one. They were still our children, of course, but we began to see them as partners as well.

Since then, we've continued to branch out, through the garden centre, then through books, catalogues, speaking engagements— even a website. And our roots remain as strong as ever. ✑

...well worth the effort...

Squash

WE ALWAYS LEFT SQUASH in the garden as late in the fall as we could, to get the best growth possible. While preparing for bed one night, we heard on the radio that a severe frost was expected. So we raced out to the field, using the headlights of our pickup trucks to light our way. We ran through the rows, searching for ripe squash, trying to save as much fruit as we could. We actually managed to save most of the squash, despite stumbling over each other in the dark. Although it was fun, I generally recommend more conventional harvesting methods.

My grandchildren Kathryn and Michael never need to be forced to help us harvest squash. They love to scavenge under the leaves to discover the fruit hidden beneath—like a treasure hunt. Perhaps the many different shapes and colours of squash are what they find so appealing.

Ready to harvest

Summer squash should be harvested when it's young and tender, since it tends to lose its rich flavour at maturity. Harvest summer squash regularly to keep the vines producing; I often harvest twice a week. Summer squash doesn't keep well, so eat it as soon as you harvest it.

It's easy to tell when winter squash is ready: if you can't pierce the skin with a fingernail, it's time to pick the fruit. You can also harvest it when all the vines have died, or after the first light frost. Cut the vines with a butcher knife, leaving some stem on the fruit. (Without some stem, the fruit won't keep and will quickly rot.) Winter squash can be stored on a shelf in a cool, dry place, but it should never be stored in an unheated garage or on a cement floor: storing squash here will lead to rot.

Be careful when cutting the tough-skinned winter squashes. Ted uses a cleaver to open squash, since we once broke a knife trying to cut one! After you get to the delicious inner flesh, though, you'll be glad you made the effort. I cook squash by steaming it between two layers of tin foil on a cookie sheet in the oven—it's a lovely treat. Our family eats a lot of squash—we feel it's a vastly underrated vegetable. Ted and I will even eat the skin, if it's been prepared properly.

Zucchini

Zucchini is a summer squash that's finally getting its due. I say bravo! It's about time! Pick zucchini when it's small, young, and tender—it's at its best when it's no more than 20 cm long. When you can pierce the skin easily with your nail, you've got a nice, ripe zucchini.

Commercial growers harvest their zucchini every other day, since this vegetable becomes oversized and inedible quicker than any other. The best size for zucchini is about the same as a small slicing cucumber. In fact, at the wholesale level, zucchini prices plunge as the fruit gets larger—to the point where it becomes completely unsaleable.

My daughter-in-law Valerie likes to cut zucchini lengthwise, into long, thin strips. She adds cheddar, salt and pepper, and a sprinkling of chopped green onions, heats it in the oven, and serves. It's a simple and tasty treat that she says "even men can make."

Squash of Choice: Warted Hubbard

Also known as Green Hubbard, this is my family's favourite squash. It's a winter type with dark-green skin and sweet, dry, orange flesh.

Squash seeds need warm soil to germinate, so I sow from late May to early June, 5 seeds per hill. A single plant can produce over 7 kg of summer squash, or 10 kg of winter squash.

...gorgeous orange ripeness...
Pumpkin

For us, a pumpkin is much more than just another garden-variety vegetable. Growing a large, orange pumpkin by harvest time has come to symbolize an exceptionally good season. In our climate, we grow a lot of green pumpkins, but few reach that gorgeous orange shade that signifies full ripeness. When they do, it means we've had lots of rain, warm weather, and a long fall. And who can imagine Halloween without jack-o'-lanterns leering from their haunts on creaky wooden porches and dusty windowsills?

When I grow pumpkins in the family garden, I always plant seedlings into rich, well-drained soil in a sheltered, sunny spot. I water and fertilize the plants heavily throughout the growing season. To give myself a better shot at getting some ripe pumpkins by season's end, I pick off all new blossoms after three or four fruits have formed on each plant. With the plant's resources devoted to just a few fruit, those that remain are more likely to reach large sizes and full ripeness.

Orange Yellow is...

Orange is a pumpkin, ripe and shining
That we eat in our pumpkin pie.
Yellow is the glow and warmth of the candle,
After we've had our fill.
Yellow is the sun shining on the leaves,
Glowing a golden glow.
Orange is a young tomato,
Shooting into full growth.
Yellow is the glow of the morning sun,
When the bats go to sleep,
uʍop ǝpᴉsdn

—Kathryn Hole. age 8

Another happy accident

In 1998, we filled many of our pots in the greenhouse with compost that included leftover pumpkins from the previous year. Little did we know that many of the pumpkin seeds had survived the heat of the rotting compost, so a number of the potted plants that we sold eventually wound up producing a little—or not-so-little—bonus for the consumer. One business owner bought a large barrel of petunias and trained the pumpkin vine to grow up the side of his building. (He had to trim the fruits off, of course, since their weight would have dragged the vine off the building.) We went out to see it when he called us, and it really looked great. He was just beaming with pride. You know, I never would have thought of growing pumpkins in a petunia pot—but once again, life's little accidents showed us something new.

Pumpkin of Choice: Spirit

These bright-orange beauties typically reach sizes of 7 kg. They are perfect for carving and make tasty pies.

I plant seedlings in mid-May, three seedlings in each hill. Pumpkins require a lot of space, so you will need to thin the seedlings. In an ideal growing season, eight hills will produce about 45 kg of pumpkin, enough for several jack-o'-lanterns and a rack of pumpkin pies.

❦ We call it a pumpkin. In French, it's *potiron*; in German, *Zentnerkürbis*; in Spanish, *calabaza grande*; in Italian, *zucca invernale*.

...an irresistible challenge...

Melons

WE ONCE TRIED TO GROW melons commercially. Our melons were babied: we planted them in areas where they would get the most heat and shelter, used different kinds of plant covers to create heat-trapping mini-greenhouses, gave them the right amounts of water and fertilizer, and removed blossoms after three or four fruits had formed per plant. Even so, yields were so low that the crop wasn't commercially viable. However, we learned enough to grow melons pretty successfully on a small scale, so we enjoy them fresh from our own garden every year.

There's nothing like the feeling you get when you manage to grow melons successfully. Since they're heat-loving plants, I find the challenge of growing them in cool northern gardens hard to resist.

Try it yourself

In 1998, Ted piled up mounds of not-quite-rotted compost into which my daughter-in-law Valerie planted melons. The heat produced by the degrading compost keeps the roots warm. She had to add more fertilizer than usual, since the composting process draws

❀ Melons are ancient, having been cultivated, as far as we can determine, since prehistoric times. Their popularity continues today: in Egypt, watermelon seeds are as favoured as sunflower seeds are here.

a lot of nitrogen from the soil, but the added heat was worth the extra expense. The melons took off in this environment.

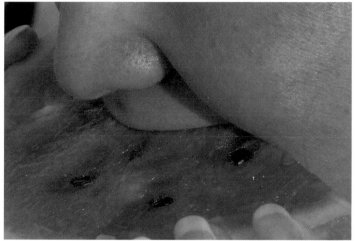

In Montana, it's common to draw a heat-retaining blanket over melon plants each night. Like all warm-weather crops, melons respond to this treatment with more vigorous growth. As average daily temperatures climb, the growth rate increases until temperatures reach the mid-30s, where the growth curve levels off. Simply put, the more heat you give your melons, the better they will do.

Melon of Choice: Alienor

As the name suggests, this cantaloupe is out of this world. The succulent orange flesh smells wonderful and tastes even better.

Melons must be transplanted into northern gardens because of the short growing season. Do this only after all danger of frost has passed. Each plant will probably produce 3 or 4 good-sized melons.

❀ Melons should never be refrigerated: they lose their flavour and texture quickly. Keep them at room temperature instead.

There are two ways to learn: by studying and by doing. There's an unfortunate tendency among many people to favour one and dismiss the other—some feel that experience is the best teacher, while others put their faith in books alone. If there's anything I've discovered over the years, it's that both kinds of education are necessary for success.

Next to the right soil, a gardener's most valuable resources are knowledge and experience. If you don't have any of your own, you should be prepared to draw on the knowledge and experience of others. Often, the best way to do this is to buy a book.

When we were just starting out in the market gardening business, Ted and I relied on books for our very survival. Ted had never lived on a farm and didn't have any relatives who farmed. His mother didn't even grow much of a garden. My mom had instilled in me a love of gardening, but I knew I still had a lot to learn. After all, this was no hobby, it was our livelihood.

Having earned his degree in agriculture, Ted had a great deal of technical knowledge. We also found some wonderful books to help us translate that knowledge into good gardening practice. If we wanted to know when to plant a certain crop or how deep to sow the seeds, we'd look it up. Sometimes we'd study the books at the kitchen table over a cup of coffee, making notes to bring along with us when we went out to work.

This left us open to a little teasing from the neighbours. Most of them were much older than we were, and they believed the only way to learn to grow something was by going out and doing it. If you wanted to plant corn, well, go out and plant corn. It made them

chuckle to see Ted out there, poring over the notes in his diary. "There stands an expert in his field," they'd say.

It was tough sometimes, being teased by people who obviously had a lot more experience than we did. But it also made us work that much harder. And as a result, we often had the last laugh.

We looked upon those books as instruction manuals. For instance, we read that corn has very shallow roots and that it has a particular fondness for phosphorus. Then we knew that if we watered regularly and chose the proper fertilizer, the yields from our corn crop would be much greater.

And because of the books, we often planted crops much earlier than our neighbours. Instead of planting on the May long weekend, which is what most people did, we'd check the book. It would give us suggested dates for planting and tell us which plants could withstand a bit of frost. Skeptical looks from the neighbours eventually gave way to admiring gazes at our bountiful early crops.

Basic, practical knowledge like that could take a lifetime to develop on your own. But if you read books, ask questions, and take a few chances, you'll be amazed at the results. Even now, I learn something new about gardening almost every day.

People often tell me that they take my gardening books out to the garden with them. I'm pleased that my writing can be put to such immediate, practical use, especially when I think back to Ted in the field with his books. If I can do for gardeners what those old books did for us, my work has been more than worthwhile.

Left page:

...foot on a cliff shattered with loose debris...

...we had an anxious climb of 900 feet up glaciated... we then descended two feet to Dais... we looked the lake at least, and its... to the publishing to the leader at least, and its... would yawn to a region where glacial features are... and round the base of the cliffs everywhere are... the upper lip, and finally we had to cross a slen-... ice slope to steep rocks, where a shower of... crampons with one hand while hanging...

...We went straight up to... the ledges sloping. Much of the south face of... peak about 1000 feet high. Much of the... ...advance along it was not perhaps impossible... the dignity of individual peaks...

...were now level with the top of Dais Glacier, about... ...south wall of the Mystery Mountain, crowned... ...imposing blue cliffs of Epaulette Glacier. Forest...

...the descent was the glaciated slabs above our biv... at 4,500 p.m. The tedious tramp back to Icefall Point... cliff-foot capped by a lively hanging glacier on the...

...went on the 9th to base camp and brought up... broke and we found our camp site very bleak.

...orridor Glacier, the east branch of Mystery... ...all Point. Finding the ice much shattered... ...imbed the cliffs 350 feet to a small grass... a little rain would have made it un-... handful of juniper sticks helped out... ...ur packs.

...a.m., descending to the broken... ...g out to the middle where the... ...d by thin, brittle snow. At... ...e mound at the foot of the... all on Buckler Glacier by... ...face of Mystery Moun-

Right page:

...sin. Richly violet the shadow of the earth hung in the southwesterly sky under a band of glowing rose so vivid it might well have been the sun's van-guard instead of night's rearguard.

The massive ruins of the icefall were a delight to the eye, but serious obstacles. More than once a single bridge was the only possible route in the whole width of the ice. To avoid passing immediately ...pling 100-foot glaciers we were forced to find a way up a succession of ...der the hanging walls, and we crossed the glacier three times among ...ir immense frag-ments before we ...ing over S...way to the basin abov...awny smoke-clouds were now po...Monday from the north...

The sunlight had struck the upper face of Mystery Mountain and the great precipices reverberated with loosened ...s and ice and snow. Most of the southerly face is so swept by ...Spearman Peak [now know... ...s Spearman Peak] and tinctly rounded off.

We hoped...

...the snow slope on... Crest of the easter... Mystery Mountain and the ...ence of this eas... ...en Peak as ...oking ridge. ...that the edges of ledges are dis-...ly mottled ...face of ...ridge by way of a belt of cliffs ...t baffling with several colours from ...Spearmen Peak which guards clim...t where it ...mouflage giving the mis...re ...more or so." The rocks are schist ...reak with n...holly impossible. The nea... ...nearly black; the effect ...e tried thre...erous small overhangs. ...ve ...vertical slabs of granite the ex...e as the h...easy looking ways, the last one being ...rve-racking in ...ll. ...ed with blood, and ...t of the day was bringing down ...now ...rocks along rock...from her sister's head...were bruised repeatedly; M...Mur...s hair was vanced would have violated the...r arm severely bruised by ...tering it toward a Therefore we started down...inally a place was rea...ed where to have ad-...had not yet strengthened the snow ...mentary Princ...les of good climbing. collapsing. When we had groped an anxious wa...bergschrund at dusk. Frost icefall, the moon topped Spearman Peak. Steep slopes b...the worst of the come especially trying as the frosty crust broke away fro...his time h... below. Four hours were required to descend ...reached the bivouac at 3:45 a.m.

Shortly past noon we were n...
6:55 p.m., having decided to descend...
dable west ridge which...
the summit.

...something almost magical...

Tomatoes

WE ONCE PLANTED A LARGE PATCH of tomatoes right next to our house, on a south-facing wall. As usual, we planted extra, since it wasn't unusual for only a portion of the crop to come to fruition. Wouldn't you know it—the season turned out to be perfect! The summer was long and hot, with just the right amount of moisture. As a result, we wound up with tons of tomatoes, more than we could ever hope to use or sell. One day, a friendly Italian man was driving by and spotted the tomato motherlode. With a grin, he offered to take away any extras we had. Well, we filled the box of his 1958 Chevy half-ton right to the brim. He told us he was going to make the load into sauce— surely enough to last a lifetime! A tomato or two bounced out of the back of the truck as he drove off with a happy wave. I've always believed that no other vegetable can produce such spontaneous joy in people; there's just something magical about tomatoes.

A good start

Tomatoes need a lot of care, and choosing a location for them is just the first step. I always make sure to give them one of the garden "hot spots," along our south-facing wall. With our climate, I put transplants into the garden, and I always use top-quality plants. Buying poor plants never makes sense; use good quality plants that are sure to bear lots of fruit rather than poor plants that won't yield well. I always ensure that the plants have been "hardened off," that is, acclimatized to the harsher conditions they will face outdoors. Plants that haven't been properly hardened off will be set back.

I'm alert to cool night-time temperatures and ready to run to the rescue when necessary. If there is any threat of frost, I cover the plants with blankets or towels: tomatoes simply can't take the cold. (Never use plastic—it's a poor insulator.)

I use cages for my determinate (bush) tomato plants. Although it isn't strictly necessary, I find these plants benefit from the use of cages, since bush tomato plants tend to spread across the ground. The foliage becomes quite thick and bushy, protecting the fruit from sun scald, but fruit often lay on the ground. Cages hold the fruit off the soil, decreasing the threat of slugs and soil-borne diseases. Tall-growing indeterminate tomato plants, of course, must be staked and pruned.

Caring for tomatoes may be demanding work, but biting into the sweet, red fruit makes it all worth while.

Fruit of Choice: Tumbler

By now, everyone has probably heard me rave about Tumbler tomatoes, but I just can't help myself—this is the best tomato I've ever grown. The plant produces high yields (counts of 300 fruit on one plant are not uncommon) of delightful, mid-size tomatoes.

I transplant seedlings during the last two weeks of May. Tumblers are heavy feeders and need lots of water and fertilizer. A selection of paste, slicing, and cherry tomatoes will provide fruit for salads, cooking, canning, and eating off the vine from late June through September.

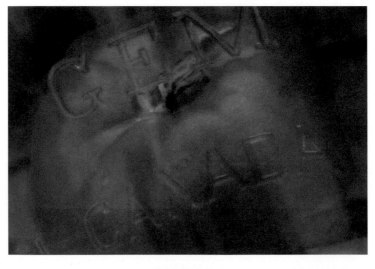

❧ I've heard tomatoes called the canaries of the garden, because they are so sensitive to misapplication of herbicides. Keep this in mind when you're thinking of using chemicals to control weeds close to tomatoes.

❧ Tomatoes should be picked early to avoid over-ripening. If you wait until they are fully red, the fruits have already begun to soften, and can be mushy and less tasty.

Can We Go Yet?

A WOMAN CAME OUT to our farm one day with her two little boys. They were really cute kids, but were they active! After telling her sons over and over, "Don't touch! Stop running! Leave that alone!", she had finally had enough. "Listen up," she snapped, "if you kids don't start behaving, I'm gonna leave you here!"

If Grandma Hole had been there, she would have said, "Never threaten your kids unless you plan to carry it out." Calmly, but firmly, I jumped in: "Oh no you're not!"

No matter how much you love children, if you're in any kind of retail business you have a few horror stories about them (and their parents). With experience, you learn to intervene tactfully and stop trouble before it starts. But that experience does not come easily.

When we first started in the greenhouse business, we kept our bedding plants on the floor. Because they were within reach of little fingers, the plants often lost a few leaves or blossoms. One little boy had no interest in the plants themselves. He was more intrigued by the identification tags with their colourful pictures. He went quietly along, carefully pulling them out of the packs of petunias. By the time he was caught, he had a tidy collection of 200 or so. The plants were ready for sale, but suddenly we had no way of telling what colour the flowers would be. We had to hold onto all of those petunias for an extra couple of weeks while we waited for them to bloom. In the meantime, we lost dozens of sales.

This boy was old enough to have known better, but we also had to accept our share of the blame. If kids are bored, they're going to look around for something to do. If all they see is a bunch of plants, they'll find a way to have fun with them.

There's a very simple, two-part solution for making kids behave in this kind of situation. First, if you don't want kids to touch something, for heaven's sake keep it out of their reach. Our plants have been up on tables for many years now, safe and sound. Second, make sure kids have something interesting to do.

In our market gardening days, we encouraged children to play in our yard while their parents shopped. The moment a customer's car stopped in our driveway, the doors would spring open. Boys and girls would pile out and race across the yard to climb in the trees or play on the rope swing —a wonderful sight! When we designed our current garden centre, we saved room for an outdoor play area, including a slide, teeter-totter, and other playground toys.

Even so, with the amount of time they spend following patiently along while their parents shop, it's no wonder some children lose control. When I spot the danger signs, I walk over and put a plant in each mischievous hand. "Here's a present for you," I tell them. "Take them home and plant them in your garden." They walk around with their plants, as proud as can be, and they can't touch another thing.

Best of all, this little trick helps the parents feel calmer and happier too. As a result, they never even think of leaving their beautiful children behind! ✀

A Steward of the Land

WHEN I OPENED my front door to Mr. Atkinson one evening long ago, I had no idea who he was. He explained that he lived across the way and had noticed us moving in. "How nice," I thought. "Our new neighbours are already making us feel welcome." But Mr. Atkinson had a more serious purpose in mind.

Mr. Atkinson was a missionary, but not the sort you usually find on your doorstep. He came knocking to spread the gospel of trees. Ever since he had arrived in Canada from England, he had been concerned about the local environment. In the rush to clear the land, he felt, Canada's early farmers had forgotten the importance of trees. Over time, he had made it his goal to encourage people to replant trees on the landscape.

Back then, most farmers looked on trees as rivals, taking up land that could be put to more "productive" use. Mr. Atkinson was very active in the farmers' union and used it as a forum to spread the word. He showed farmers that trees, properly placed, could actually improve their crop yields and protect the rich prairie soil from eroding winds.

In those days, you could get little saplings for free from our local municipality. That certainly made it easier for us to follow Mr. Atkinson's advice. Even if you have to go out and buy them, though, trees are still a wonderful investment. A shelter belt can reduce wind and capture heat, creating a microclimate that can have a positive effect on an entire field—like the one that shel-

tered our beautiful cucumbers. Mr. Atkinson also firmly believed that rows of trees would attract rainfall. Now, decades later, numerous studies suggest that he was right.

Most importantly, though, he felt spiritually drawn to trees. By planting trees, he said, you ensure that you leave the earth better than you found it. After all, what in this world is lovelier than a tree?

Not surprisingly, the Atkinsons' place was gorgeous to look at. Every morning, sitting at the breakfast table, Ted and I would watch their dairy cows being let out into the field. They'd wander peacefully along through the trees in the early morning light. It's a picture I still hold in my heart.

Anytime you chatted with Mr. Atkinson, you could bet he would raise the subject of trees. As a result, in addition to the trees he planted himself, I'm sure there are thousands more growing in Alberta thanks to him. Ted planted dozens of trees on our farm, and to this day he keeps an eye out for new species to add to his collection. He's certainly not alone. If you take aerial photos of our district from 40 years ago, and contrast them with more recent ones, you'll see Mr. Atkinson's influence.

When my boys were growing up, whenever I told them the story of Johnny Appleseed, I would add a little local touch. "Johnny Appleseed," I told them, "was a lot like Mr. Atkinson." ❧

Let Them Eat Bread And Cheese

As a gardener, I'm proud of my role as a provider of nourishment to plants and people alike. In both cases, I know the nutrients I provide help them thrive.

I feed my plants a well-balanced diet, including such elements as peat moss, bone meal, manure, compost, and fertilizer. More often than not, I'm rewarded with a thick patch of healthy, thriving plants, and the pleasure this brings me is immense.

It's even more fulfilling to provide for the people in my life. Of course, the diet's a bit different! I keep a bowl of fresh fruit in the middle of my kitchen table and include plenty of vegetables with our meals. And when all else fails, I make sure to maintain a steady supply of bread and cheese.

One blistering August day, Ted and I emerged from the fields sweaty, grimy, and exhausted. We dragged ourselves into the house and flopped onto the living-room sofa. After a little rest, we cleaned ourselves up and prepared for a quiet, relaxing evening together.

Just as we were settling down with a couple of good books and some pleasant music on the radio, there was a knock on the door. Ted and I looked at each other wide-eyed, both instantly remembering that we'd invited some friends over for dinner. We'd completely forgotten!

"Stall them!" I whispered to Ted, rushing into the kitchen.

While Ted greeted our friends at the door and held them off with small talk, I frantically rummaged through the cupboards for food. We had several bottles of wine—housewarming gifts that we'd been stockpiling—but our larder was practically empty. But as always, there was a good supply of bread and cheese. I set it on the table with a hastily tossed salad, and opened some wine.

I went out to the porch to invite our guests inside. We served the meal as if it was what we'd planned, and they were perfectly happy with that. Eventually, Ted and I admitted we'd forgotten all about our dinner plans, and everyone had a good laugh.

Over the years, bread and cheese has become something of a personal trademark. If the kids were late going to school in the morning, I'd give them bread and cheese to eat on the way. If we had unexpected visitors, I never hesitated to invite them to stay for lunch; even if there weren't enough potatoes in the pot, I knew they could always eat bread and cheese.

I can be an absolute tyrant about eating properly. Years ago, our niece Donna came to stay with us. Like most teenagers, she liked sleeping in and would often try to dash out the door without slowing down for breakfast. I never let her get away with it. If she was going to live in our house, she was darn well going to eat three square meals a day. There was lots of grumbling, a little resistance, but once she began eating regular, healthy meals, Donna could tell the difference. She felt more alert and had more energy throughout the day.

Many of our staff members at the greenhouse come to work without a good breakfast. There's nothing I can do about that, but I can help them catch up a little later in the day.

We've always tried to keep the lunchroom stocked with snacks—bagels and cream cheese, or toast and jam. My Auntie Anne often came to the farm loaded down with fresh baking for the staff. After a couple of hours on the job, especially doing physical labour, a body gets desperate for some fuel, and people know they can always grab a little something on their breaks. When they get back to work, they're happier, more energetic, and having more fun.

❧❧❧

Sometimes I wish we lived in a less hectic world, where everyone could find time to enjoy a simple breakfast. I hate to see people going hungry. It hurts, especially when there's no need for it. We are rich enough to feed everyone, and yet, somehow, we're not quite smart enough or fair enough to do it.

When Bill and Jim were young, they had a classmate who would ask, very timidly, for their leftovers. When I discovered that this was going on, my heart just broke. I started packing the boys' lunches with extra food, more than they could possibly eat. When this boy approached them, Bill and Jim always had an extra sandwich and an apple they could give him.

I still wonder about that boy. I hope that his family's circumstances improved, that he's leading a full life today. I hope…but I'm not convinced. Sometimes, the little we do just isn't enough.

But that doesn't mean we should stop trying. During our market garden years, we made large donations of vegetables to the Salvation Army and other charitable groups. And we weren't the only ones. I remember that each year, one outstanding citizen would send us a cheque for $1,000 to buy vegetables for the poor. He never let us use his name—"just make sure that the people who need it get this food," he said.

If you are able to afford to eat well, for goodness' sake take advantage of it. Here, in the midst of plenty, too many folks choose to eat junk—if they eat at all! A good, healthy meal doesn't have to be complicated and it doesn't need to take a lot of time. If you feed your body well, it will reward you.

It's one way we can make the world a happier, healthier, more productive place. If you have food to spare, set some aside for your fellow humans. And no matter how busy life gets, slow down once in awhile for a proper meal.

Even if it's just bread and cheese. ❧

Listen to the Radio

IF OUR LIFE WERE made into a movie, the soundtrack would be CBC radio. From our very earliest days on the farm, the radio has provided us with company, entertainment, information, and a link to the rest of the world.

I think of the long days we spent in the bottom of the barn, cutting seed potatoes. Without the radio, the job would have been painfully monotonous. Instead, it's one of my warmest memories. Thanks to the CBC, the air was filled with voices and stories from across the country. We would cut and chop, chatting about whatever show happened to be on, and before we knew it, the job was done.

In the early days, before the children were born, I often found myself alone on the farm. Ted, a plumber by trade, would spend his days in Edmonton throughout the winter, while I stayed home and did chores. I never felt isolated, though. With the radio playing all day, I knew what was going on in the world.

As the boys grew up, I liked the idea that they were so well informed. They were always eager to discuss current events, and they formed strong political opinions long before they were old enough to vote. Of course, if they were working alone, they'd usually switch over to a rock 'n' roll station if the program didn't interest them. But over time, they've come to appreciate the CBC as much as we do.

We relied on the CBC for vital information, like weather forecasts and farm reports, but its presence was far more pervasive than that. At the breakfast table, we'd hear the national anthem right before the day's first newscast at 5:30 a.m. On most Saturday afternoons, you could find the boys laughing uproariously at some comedy show. In bed, before drifting off to sleep, we could listen to classical music.

When an important news story broke, we always heard it first on the CBC. Even though we lived on a farm, we felt connected to events around the globe. I'll never forget the day we were working in the barn and the announcer cut in to say that President Kennedy had been shot. For the rest of the day, we followed that awful story, glued to the radio.

The CBC remains a huge part of our lives. If I give a gardening talk out of town, I do my best to be finished and back in my car by 9:00 p.m. That way, I can drive home listening to *Ideas* with Lister Sinclair. In the kitchen, as I prepare the noon meal, *This Morning* keeps me company (although I must admit I miss Peter Gzowski). I believe in learning something new every day, and the CBC makes that not only possible but inevitable.

You can imagine the excitement I felt the first time I appeared on a CBC show! Without the CBC, my life would have been much poorer in so many ways. It's truly worth celebrating. ❧

The New Girl

VISITORS TO OUR GREENHOUSE often compliment us on the innovative varieties we introduce every year. If I have time, I take them out to our wonderful trial garden, for a peek at some of the varieties we'll be offering the next spring. And I always tell them a little story about the woman in charge of that garden.

One summer, an eleven-year old girl named Valerie came to work for us. She wanted a job to earn enough money to buy a new trail bike. On her first morning, we took her up to the field and left her in the pea patch to pick, promising to come back for her later in the day.

That afternoon, Ted was changing a tire on the John Deere 1020 tractor. The axle fell and came down on his leg, breaking it badly. He was a mess. We bundled him into the truck and headed for the nearest hospital, in Edmonton. In the confusion, we completely forgot about Valerie. She stayed up in that field, wondering when someone would check on her and feeling lonely—and slightly annoyed—as the hours dragged on.

Finally, around 6:00 p.m., she wandered down on her own and found the farm abandoned. She rode home in a fury. Her mother asked how her first day of work had gone.

"They stuck me up in a pea patch all day and no one came to check on me. They just left me there! I'm never going back again!"

"Calm down," her mother told her. "You can't quit a job on the first day. Something must have happened. Please go back tomorrow and try again." Little did Valerie's mom know what the happy results of this advice would be.

As the days went by and I got to know Valerie better, I realized this girl was exceptional. Smart as all get-out, a hard worker, nice looking—she could even cook a little. In short, she was a mother-in-law's dream!

So, year after year, I made sure to rehire her, and every year she came back. Soon, during our u-pick period, Valerie was the one driving people out to the fields. She later went on to university, and we still kept hiring her. And my son Bill kept right on ignoring her. Sometimes, when you plant something, it seems to take forever for it to flower.

Finally—finally!—he noticed. And he married her.

Now, if you don't think that's an arranged marriage, I have news for you! ✑

A Change of Heart

MOST OF US ARE ABLE to embrace change as an inevitable part of our lives. Everybody, however, has certain ideas or habits that they find difficult to give up. For instance, you might willingly quit your job and move out of town, but recoil in terror at the thought of trying a new hairstyle.

I like to think of myself as adaptable. Certainly, over the years, my life has undergone some major upheavals, and I've forged ahead in the belief that things almost always turn out for the best. From time to time, though, I've been known to dig in my heels. Like the day Ted suggested we start growing our bedding plants and vegetable seedlings without soil.

Ted, with his university background, always took pride in keeping up with horticultural developments. He had seen studies on raising seedlings in soil-less mixes and suggested it was time for us to give it a try.

I thought the idea was nonsense and didn't hesitate to say so. If we did manage to get the seeds to germinate, I argued, the plants wouldn't do well. Surely we needed at least some soil in our mix.

Along with his research, however, Ted had some persuasive arguments in his favour. Pasteurizing our own soil each year was a monumental task. We'd have to gather it in the fall and store it under cover. Then, beginning in January, we'd put it through our electric pasteurizer, load after load after load. It was a terribly monotonous job. Not only was this a lot of work, Ted pointed out, but with each load we were gradually depleting our own land. And if we took only soil that had washed into the ditches, he said, we could never be sure what chemicals it might contain. We didn't use a lot of herbicides or pesticides, but we had no control over others.

Sometimes, though, all the logic in the world can't move your heart. I found myself thinking of that first visit to the farm, when Ted squeezed the soil in his hand. Since then, that good earth had sustained us through thick and thin. It felt like a betrayal to turn our backs on all of that.

Deep down, I think, I also worried that the change would force me to rely more on the expertise of others. I understood how to work with soil, but this new technology was, at the time, beyond me.

So, naturally, I fought against it, but subtly, trying to bring Ted around to my point of view. "Here," I'd say, as Ted was making up the mix, "let's just add a little bit of soil." But Ted didn't listen to me. Neither did the plants. They did beautifully in the soil-less mix. Their roots spread thickly throughout the soft, even mixture, and there was no threat of soil-borne chemicals or disease.

Eventually, I had the wisdom to admit I was wrong. Once I did that, life became so much easier. We didn't have to haul and pasteurize all that soil, and the flats of seedlings weighed a fraction of what they had before.

I also recognized that, by drawing on the expertise of others, I was expanding my own knowledge and abilities. I've even taken an active role in developing, testing, and refining soil-less mixes for a wide range of uses. Since then, I've also been less afraid to try other new ideas, no matter how strange they might seem initially.

I still have a close connection to the soil. There's nothing I like better than going out to my garden on a fine day and getting my hands good and dirty.

And sometimes, on a cold, grey February afternoon, I miss the warm, earthy smell of the pasteurizing machine. Most people would find it unpleasant, but it always made me feel like spring was right around the corner.

Would I go back to those days? Not on your life. I'm happy to hold onto the pleasant memories, now that we've done away with the harsh realities. Maybe that's the nicest thing about change. ✃

...nothing like a fresh pod...

Peas

GATHERING FRESH GARDEN PEAS is one of the greatest joys I know. There's nothing like cracking open a fresh pod and popping those sweet green peas into your mouth. Unfortunately, there are no guarantees in gardening; sometimes the harvest you're hoping for isn't the one you get.

A few years ago, a sudden downpour turned into a hailstorm. The storm was brief but intense. The sun reappeared shortly, so Ted, Jim, and I went out to inspect the peas. Back then, we had to climb a rather steep hill behind our old house to reach the vegetable garden. As we climbed up, rivers of water rushed down to meet us. At first, the water was clear...then it was filled with hailstones...then with shredded pea leaves. Well, we knew then that the crop was probably destroyed, and sure enough, we reached the patch to find the plants flattened. Coincidentally, the hailstones were about the same size as peas—but not nearly as tasty!

Get them in the ground

The sooner you sow peas, the better: I throw seed into the ground as soon as it has thawed. Those cool, early spring days actually encourage the plants to grow taller and develop more pods, with

more peas in each pod. Peas are most comfortable at around 20°C, and they don't like really hot temperatures. Planting early gives you a good chance at harvesting the peas before those sweltering summer days; and until they blossom, the plants can stand nearly any frosts that happen to hit.

A lot of people soak seeds in an attempt to speed germination, but there's no real advantage to this; you're just wasting your time. Peas actually germinate better when they're simply placed in moist, loose soil.

I always pick young peas: they're of better quality than peas that have been left on the vine for weeks. Once the pods have begun to wrinkle, the peas are losing their flavour and tenderness—just like people, they wrinkle as they get older! I prefer to sacrifice yield for flavour.

Pod of Choice: Patriot

This great early-maturing variety has a very sweet taste. The plants are double-podded (two pods are produced at each flower instead of one), meaning heavier yields and more peas for dinner!

As soon as I can get into the garden, I sow a mixture of shelling, snow, and sugar snap peas. I'll be able to enjoy peas all summer, because they mature at different times. A 3 m row will yield about 4.5 kg of peas.

❦ According to Scandinavian myth, Thor, the god of thunder, once punished his people by sending dragons to drop thousands and thousands of peas upon them. The peas were meant to block up the wells so the people couldn't get any water. The plan worked, and the people suffered from thirst while the wells were being cleared. But many peas fell onto the earth and grew there, giving us a tasty new vegetable.

...handle with care...

Beans

Beans are usually one of the last vegetables I sow. They need heat; without it, they'll rot in the earth. I know I usually say plant as soon as you can work the soil, but beans are one of the exceptions to this rule. You can take a chance, but go cautiously: wait until the earth is beginning to warm, then sow thickly with treated seed (seed coated with a mild fungicide that prevents decay).

Beans are prone to producing "blind" or impotent seedlings if the seed is handled roughly. The seed coat can crack, injuring the embryo or germ. The two cotyledon leaves emerge from the ground as usual, but the plant won't grow beyond that point. I've seen this many times in the field, so remember to handle your bean seed with care!

Growing beans commercially posed a real challenge for us. The mature pods are so fragile, and we didn't have the facilities to process them quickly. They're susceptible to rust and decay, which can spread like wildfire through damp stored beans. And they're labour-intensive—they must be hand-picked to get high-quality produce. We tried automating bean-picking with a Pixall bean harvester, but went back to hand-picking. The harvester worked–and sounded—like a giant vacuum: it broke many pods and stripped their tops. The beans then needed to be sorted to remove bruised and damaged pods. The harvester was also a one-pass system, whereas hand-picking allowed us to return to the plants again and again.

❧ When storing beans, don't wash or cut the ends until you're ready to use them: doing so will make the beans mushy and encourage the spread of rust.

❧ The Greek physician Hippocrates warned that beans could injure eyesight. Even fortune-tellers would not eat them for fear of impairing their visions of the future.

❧ Never walk through a bean patch when it's wet or dewy: you'll spread disease fast! We always work in the bean patch after lunch.

We also had to watch our u-pick customers, to keep them out of the beans when they were wet. Wet bean plants are extremely vulnerable to disease and damage.

A broad range of uses

Over the years, customers from many different cultural backgrounds have visited the greenhouse. From them, I've learned about new kinds of vegetables, and new ways of using old favourites. For example, I had never thought of eating the pod from a broad bean until the Lebanese started asking for small, young broad beans, which they ate whole. The Italians, on the other hand, always asked for the largest beans, which they shelled and sautéed in olive oil.

Pod of Choice: Straight 'N Narrow

A real gourmet bush bean, this green beauty boasts absolutely outstanding size, taste, and texture. It's great as a salad bean and can be steamed, cooked, or pickled.

I like to plant a variety of bush, broad, and pole beans. For a steady supply, I often sow three times: in late May, early June, and mid June. (If I plant any earlier, I use treated seed.)

Seeds & Seeding

In addition to the right soil, the successful gardener needs to start with high-quality seeds. One spring, years ago, we noticed that mice had gotten into our corn seed. The seeds still looked more or less intact, so we decided to plant them. We waited. And we waited. Nothing grew. Unfortunately, we hadn't been dealing with ordinary mice—those mice were gourmets! Instead of eating a seed whole, they had nibbled away the germ, the part the seed needs to grow. By the time we realized our mistake, it was too late. We had no corn that summer.

Before you go to the trouble of planting, be sure of your seeds. It's worth it to use the best and freshest seed available. If you're going to devote all your time and energy to something, you should be willing to invest in it at the start, to ensure all your hard work will pay off.

When Ted and I were seeding, we would mark the rows by counting steps: one, two, three, sow, one, two, three, sow. Some clever crows followed us through the rows—one, two, three, peck, one, two, three, peck…. Those birds knew what they were doing! Of course we scared them off as best we could, but we knew they'd be back. Fortunately, we put down three seeds in each spot, so we'd get a crop even after the crows had eaten their share.

When we switched over to a mechanical seeder, I kept up my vigilance. I'd follow behind Ted's tractor and bang on the seeder whenever the seeds weren't coming out quickly enough. "Seed thicker, Ted, seed thicker!" I'd shout. He'd get a tolerant half-smile on his face and a twinkle in his eye, then nod and make the necessary adjustment.

Pests are always going to be a problem in your garden. Eventually, though, you have to accept—or better still, embrace—a degree of co-existence. If you seed your crops thickly, there will always be plenty to go around. Keep an eye open for animals and insects, sure, but when they cause some damage, take it in stride.

People too often lose perspective, especially when it comes to bugs. A woman came into the greenhouse one day, carrying a caterpillar in a jar. You could tell by the way she was holding the jar that she felt positively repulsed by her hostage. "What can I spray to get rid of these?" she asked.

I peered into the jar. "How many of them have you found?"

"Just this one."

"Well," I laughed, "it looks to me as if you've already gotten rid of it."

Around that same time, I went out for lunch with a friend of mine who's an absolute stickler for organic fruits and vegetables. When our salads arrived, she flew into a panic: there was a tiny caterpillar on one of the lettuce leaves. "Instead of causing such a fuss," I told her jokingly, "you should go back to the kitchen and thank the chef for buying organic lettuce."

I'm glad I was raised to be more relaxed about bugs. Even if adults are secretly terrified of creepy-crawly insects, it's terribly important not to act that way in front of children. When I was little, my mom and I used to go through the potato patch with coffee cans, picking off potato beetles by hand. I didn't particularly like the bugs, but I was certainly never afraid of them.

When we were market gardening, we had a whole field of potatoes, so the beetles had a little more leeway. On any given day, you could have gone out there and filled a dozen coffee cans easily. Even so, we sprayed only two or three times in all those years. As long as the problem was a small one, it just wasn't worth the trouble or expense.

I feel the same way about gophers. Some farmers go through the roof if they see a single gopher hole on their land. I prefer a compromise. The gophers can have a third of an acre to do with as they please. I only start to fight back when they cross the line.

If you can find it in your heart to work with nature, instead of constantly struggling against it, you're going to be a lot happier in the long run. It helps to look at things from the animals' (and even the insects') point of view. Maybe you were thinking only of yourself when you planted that new, sugar-enhanced variety of corn, but you're not the only one who finds it irresistible. Every creature has its place, after all.

So, next time you plant a row of seeds, try saying what I always say: "That's one for the birds, one for the bugs, and one for me…."

...sweet, bright-orange roots...

Carrots

WE LEARNED EARLY ON that carrots shrink quickly after harvesting, so they should be washed immediately. If you don't, dirt will get trapped in the cracks of the shrinking carrot, making it impossible to wash off.

One especially hot day, we washed and shipped our carrots to the wholesaler as usual—that is, without ice. The carrots decomposed because of the field-heat, and we had to take the load back. You can't imagine a more pungent smell! Washing the carrots in icewater before shipping quickly became mandatory.

Into the dirt

Different soil conditions can do strange things to carrots. Hard or rocky soil can cause roots to make abrupt 90° turns, resulting in L-shaped carrots. Soil with a high manure content produces hairy, bitter carrots. Overly rich soil leads to forked roots, while fluctuations in soil moisture can split roots. Both consistently dry and consistently waterlogged soils produce orange upper roots with very thin white tips. Finally, hot soil inhibits the production of beta carotene, the compound that give carrots their colour. The right soil is loose and rich, with a balanced fertilizer to supplement.

Harvest time

Look for bright-orange roots. These are a clear signal that the carrots are ready to be pulled. If you have a fall frost and the tops fall, don't abandon your carrots: the majority of the root, protected by the earth, will be fine.

One morning, during a fall harvest, it started to snow. We had most of the crop in, so we halted the harvest and decided to wait it out, figuring the snow would melt right away; after all, it was only early October. Well, we waited... and waited...and the snow just didn't go away. We lost that batch.

In our wholesale vegetable days, we sold Nantes carrots, which was an unusual choice. This "coreless" variety (so-called because while Nantes do have cores, they are much less woody than other varieties) is rarely found in supermarkets, because the carrots have a tendency to break. (Sadly, consumers almost never get the best produce in supermarkets, since the best-tasting varieties are often the most difficult to store and ship.) Nantes are the only choice, however, for the home garden.

Root of Choice: Nantes

These are my favourite carrots. They are very sweet and juicy, they never need peeling, and they mature early. For eating fresh, cooking, juicing, or desserts, there is no better variety.

I seed carrots at least three times during the year: in late April, in the third week of May, and around June 10. Some people use meadow seeding, a method in which the seed is simply cast over a wide area. This method produces high yields, but is suitable only if the plot is weed-free.

✿ We call it a carrot. In French, it's *carotte*; in Dutch, *peen*; in Italian, *carota*; in Spanish, *zanahoria*. Always a snappy snack!

Lois Hole's Cream of Cold Carrot Soup

2 medium onions
45 ml (3 tbsp.) butter
5 ml (1 tsp.) curry powder
2.5 ml (½ tsp.) dill seed
1 kg (2 lbs.) carrots (about 12 medium carrots)
1200 ml (5 cups) chicken stock
salt and pepper to taste
pinch of nutmeg
360-480 ml (1½-2 cups) heavy cream
fresh parsley or dill (for garnish)

Chop onions into coarse chunks. Sweat onions in saucepan or stock pot until translucent. Stir in curry powder and dill seed and continue cooking for 2 minutes. Slice carrots (reserving 1 for garnish). Combine carrots and onion mixture and add chicken stock. Season with salt, pepper and nutmeg. (Use salt sparingly if you've used bouillon for stock.) Cook for 30 minutes. Puree the mixture in a separate bowl in 3 or 4 batches. Chill thoroughly. Just before serving, stir in cream, adjust seasoning, and garnish each bowl with a carrot curl and a sprig of parsley or dill. Serves 6-8. **Variation:** If served hot, add the cream gradually to pureed carrot mixture and heat gently, without boiling.

Parsnips

Harvesting parsnips—a close cousin of carrots—can be quite a challenge. I remember Bill and Jim struggling to uproot them, gasping for breath when the vegetables were finally ripped from the earth. It's not unusual to have roots that extend more than two feet into the earth—sometimes three! For this reason, parsnips should be grown in loose, peaty soil: this will make it much easier to harvest the roots. Parsnips don't need rich soil, but avoid growing them in sandy soil; parsnips brown easily, and sandy soil aggravates the problem.

For goodness' sake, don't try eating parsnips raw—it'll put you off them for good! Instead, try this: bake them in the oven with some brown sugar and add some butter when serving. You'll be surprised how tasty they are!

Stirring the Soil

Gardening offers many pleasures, but weeding isn't one of them. Most successful gardeners develop their own special tricks to make the job easier, and if you coax them a bit, they'll share their secrets with you. The best weeding trick I've ever learned, however, didn't come from a friend or a book.

One spring day, Ted seeded an enormous patch of carrots, with 85 beautifully even rows. A few days later, while we were eating lunch, Ted and I noticed that our pigs seemed a bit noisier than usual. Gradually, a horrible realization sank in: the pigs were loose. Sure enough, when we looked out, we saw the whole bunch of them, rolling around in the soft, moist soil of the carrot patch.

I was just sick. Ted put on his bravest face and said, "Oh, Lois, don't worry. I'll re-seed it tomorrow." Well, of course, the next morning, rain set in and didn't let up for days. Ted never did get back to re-seeding.

A week later, I walked out to the garden. I couldn't believe my eyes. There were the rows of seedlings, as neat and straight as could be. And any place that the pigs had rolled, there were no weeds, while the places they had missed were full of tiny emerging weed seedlings.

I was ready to let the pigs out again!

When I thought about it, it made sense. While those pigs had been having their fun, they were exposing thousands of tiny weeds to the elements. Meanwhile, a half inch below the surface, the carrot seeds remained safe and sound.

It's called "stirring the soil," and you can use the same approach even if you don't have pigs. When you plant your garden, say in early April, go out with a rake about two weeks later. Turn the prongs up to the sky and go over the entire area you planted. Just move the surface soil around. You won't do any harm to your garden, but you'll kill so much chickweed, you won't believe it.

When you seed again a couple of weeks later, you should wait only seven or eight days before raking, because the soil has begun to warm up and the seeds will germinate more quickly. By late May, wait only four days. With just a few minutes' work, you can save yourself literally hours of weeding.

Ted took this trick a step farther. He always harrowed the potato field just before the plants emerged, to kill the competing weeds. He'd hitch spring-tooth harrows to the Massey Ferguson and drive along at about ten kilometres an hour, disturbing the soil as much as possible without damaging the crops. It was a great time-saver in the long run.

It goes to show you, if you pay attention, you never know what you might learn, even from pigs.

⁂

About fifteen years after the "pig incident," I gave this tip to a group of farm women. I had always thought it a remarkable pearl of wisdom. But that afternoon, an elderly woman came up to me and said, "Lois, my grandmother did that, my mother did that, and I've done that, and it works like a damn." ❧

The New Push Seeder

LIKE MOST FARMERS, Ted always kept an eye out for a new piece of equipment that would make his work more efficient. That's why I wasn't surprised when he came home with a shiny new Stanhay precision carrier-seeder one day, even though (as far as I could tell) there was nothing wrong with our old Planet Junior.

Like any kid with a new toy, Ted just couldn't wait to try it out. As he pulled on his coveralls, I eyed the seeder skeptically.

"Ted," I said, "it looks awfully heavy. How in the world will you push it through all that soft soil?"

"No problem," he laughed, heading out to the garden.

I settled back to watch him. Right away, I could see he was in trouble—his face was already getting red from the exertion as he leaned into the 50 kilogram seeder, trying to push it through the soft earth. I pulled on my boots and ran out to lend a hand.

"Ted," I said, "you take one handle and I'll take the other, and we'll push it together." We managed to seed the first row, heading down the gentle slope toward the riverbank. Then we got to the bottom and turned around to head uphill. Well, we might just as well have tried pushing the thing up Mt. Everest. It was hopeless.

After much panting and sweating, we took a break, leaning against the seeder, wondering what in the world to do. "Ted," I said, "this just isn't going to work." He was too stubborn to admit defeat, however. There was no way he was going to go back to using the old seeder after buying this new one.

He ran to the garage and fetched a long piece of rope. He wrapped it around my waist, then tied an end onto each handle of the seeder. There I was in front, with Ted holding the handles from behind.

"Lois," he said, "start walking."

I stared at him for a moment, hardly believing what I had heard. I had to admit, though, it was a good idea, and probably the only way we were going to get the field seeded. Feeling rather like a plough horse, I started pulling.

Well, it worked. We went up the row and down the row, up the row and down the row. The going wasn't too bad, really, and we actually started to enjoy ourselves. I stopped feeling silly and just got into the steady rhythm of pulling the seeder along while Ted put his back into it and pushed.

Just then, a car happened to pass by. The driver slammed on his brakes, threw the car into reverse, and pulled off on the side of the road. As we neared the fence, we saw four startled, slack-jawed faces peering at us through the car windows. I had a momentary flash of embarrassment—"Just look at their expressions!"—but then I thought, "Well, who cares what they think?" In farming, you've got to be willing to do whatever it takes.

After silently observing us for half a dozen long, long rows, the car slowly and quietly pulled away. By this time, Ted and I were killing ourselves laughing, picturing the story these folks would tell when they got back to the city.

"Lois," Ted said, "how I wish I'd had a whip!" ✌

A Woman of the Soil

PEOPLE OFTEN TELL ME they're amazed by my gardening expertise. Well, it's true I'm a pretty good gardener, but much of my knowledge comes from the advice I have gathered from others. I've had many great teachers, and one of them will always hold a special place in my memory—not just for the knowledge she passed on, but for the inspiration I took from her courage and determination.

Respected pioneer dies

A beloved St. Albert pioneer has died of complications associated with diabetes.

Virginie Durocher, 92, died Saturday, July 7 at Edmonton's Misericordia Hospital. She had been a resident at Lynnwood Auxiliary Hospital since 1988.

A resident of St. Albert for more than 40 years, Durocher lived in a two-room log cabin until 1965, when she moved to Villeneuve.

She is survived by four sons, four daughters, and more than 100 grandchildren, great grandchildren and three great-great grandchildren.

Born in Gunn, Alta. in 1898 Durocher spoke a mixture of Cree, French and English.

Although she was illiterate all her life, she was an expert on Alberta's native plants and their uses. The University of Alberta used her expertise in 1960 to identify and chart medicinal plants in this area.

Durocher worked at Hole's Greenhouses for 22 years, until she was 80

Virginie Durocher

when her children convinced her to retire.

Lois Hole remembers Durocher's expertise with plants.

"She was very knowledgeable about weeds, she knew all the medicinal uses for herbs and plants. If you had a stomach ache, she would tell you what herb to make a tea of. If you had a headache, she'd tell you to take the bark off some tree and make

a tea out of that. She even had a tonic against baldness," Hole said, laughing.

Hole remembers well the hut Durocher lived in.

"I used to pick her up every morning to take her to our farm," she said. "It was just logs and mud, with a mud floor. No running water, of course, and she kept the wood stove outside, because the house was so small. But it was always as neat and tidy as a pin."

A daughter of Durocher, Alice Wotowich remembers the log cabin fondly. She said one of the rooms was full of beds.

"There were 10 of us plus all the kids she took care of," Wotowich said. "She was always taking in kids who didn't have parents."

Prayers for Durocher will be at the St. Albert Funeral Home Wednesday, July 11 at 7 p.m. Funeral services will be held Thursday July 12 at 10 a.m. at the St. Albert Roman Catholic Church.

THE ST. ALBERT GAZETTE, WED., JULY 11, 1990 - A3

Mrs. Durocher was a Métis woman who often worked for the Gervais family, potato farmers who lived on the farm next to us. Mrs. Gervais knew I needed help with my vegetable garden, so she introduced me to Mrs. Durocher. Little did I know the impact this extraordinary woman would have on my family.

The first day she came out to our place, I was struck both by her wisdom and by her generosity of spirit. That week, cucumbers were just starting to appear on our vines. She told me that if I picked them right away, the vines would go on to produce a much heavier crop. I was a little leery of the suggestion, but decided to give it a try. Well, those plants just exploded. I had never seen so many cucumbers.

When I give that tip at gardening talks, people think I'm a genius. But it was Mrs. Durocher who taught me.

During long summer afternoons, as we worked side by side, Mrs. Durocher would tell me about the plants that grew in the area and the many uses she had for them. If you made a tea out of one plant, it would help you get over a cold. You could apply the leaves of another directly to cuts or blisters to help them heal properly. She even knew of a plant that she claimed could prevent baldness!

With the depth of her knowledge, she wasn't always ready to accept the word of "experts." When she gave birth to her first child, the doctors told her that the baby was weak and frail, and might not survive. They said there was nothing they could do. So Mrs. Durocher decided to see what she could do to help her newborn son.

Mrs. Durocher was determined to save him. She filled dozens of discarded bottles with hot water and wrapped the child in blankets, creating an incubator. That heat, warm milk, and love were all she needed to save the child.

Because we thought so highly of Mrs. Durocher, it sometimes came as a shock that she didn't think very highly of herself. I remember how excited she was when she gave birth to a son with light-coloured hair—she was thrilled that his hair wasn't pure black.

Once, Ted asked Mrs. Durocher if he could take her picture. She had the most striking, unforgettable face. Her olive skin seemed smooth, even though it was deeply lined, and her eyes radiated wisdom and character. Ted wanted to capture the image of this important part of our lives forever, and Mrs. Durocher was delighted to be asked.

When Ted visited her with the camera the next day, he discovered, to his dismay, that she had coated her long, white hair with shoe polish, trying to look young for the photo. This story always makes me sad. If only she would believe that we loved who she was and how she looked.

She truly touched the lives of everyone she came in contact with. Our greenhouse manager, Dave Grice, remembers Mrs. Durocher fondly. He started at the farm as a teenager back in the early '70s and often worked in the fields alongside her. He recalls how graceful and quiet her movements were, as if she were walking on air. Although Mrs. Durocher was 65 or 70 years old at the time, she never had a problem keeping up with the rest of the workers.

When Dave talks about Mrs. Durocher working in the field, I remember how thorough she was. She had a sixth sense about weeds and seemed never to miss a single one.

Mrs. Durocher died a few years later, and we've missed her ever since. Along with her wise, gentle presence and her unfailing good company, we also lost the opportunity to preserve her wisdom. She tended to mix her English with Cree, and I couldn't always understand her. If only I had taken the time to get somebody who could translate, to help me get it all down on paper. All that knowledge died with her. She had many children, but as far as I know, they had never taken an interest in her "old ways."

"You know," Dave told me recently, "I'm amazed at how often the image of Mrs. Durocher comes to my mind. She knew the soil like no one else I've ever known."

In this helter-skelter, technological age, people are desperate to get back to the soil. Gardening continues to boom and every supermarket has a corner devoted to organic fruits and vegetables. Even in the local pharmacy, you can find a wide range of herbal remedies squeezed in among the aspirins and toothpaste.

Mrs. Durocher would have been delighted by all this interest in nature and natural ways. It's such a shame that, in her day, her wisdom wasn't fully appreciated, not even by her.

I like to think that, if she were alive today, Mrs. Durocher's life would be very different. She would be a respected elder in the community and would feel free to take pride in her native ancestry.

After all these years, perhaps the world is finally starting to catch up with her way of thinking. I learned so much from Mrs. Durocher—and not just about gardening. ❧

Lois Says...

I'VE ALWAYS SAID TO MY FAMILY I can't believe that overnight, in the eyes of the public, I became the gardening expert! It all happened when we moved from the old barn to our modern greenhouse in the late '70s. I found myself the obvious expert, with people saying to me, "Lois, you know everything!"

꒰꒰꒰

When we hire new staff each spring, my sons Bill and Jim always give them a friendly piece of advice: "Any time a customer begins a sentence with 'Lois says...,' for heaven's sake don't argue. If you try to tell them something different, they'll only think you're trying to mislead them."

My boys chuckle about this, but to tell the truth, I find it a little unnerving. People should never treat my word like some kind of holy writ. I'm happy to give whatever advice I can, and I usually know what I'm talking about. More importantly, I've been surrounded by experts every day of my working life and can draw on their knowledge. But I'm only human. Believe it or not, I even make the occasional mistake.

One day at a gardening talk, I recommended "Rocket" tomatoes. It was one of those strange slips of the tongue: in reality, we hadn't sold Rocket tomatoes for years. Sure enough, for the next few weeks, we had people coming to the greenhouse asking for them. Even though the staff explained the error, a few customers remained adamant. If Lois said to buy Rockets, they were darn well going to buy Rockets! It took a lot of explaining to convince them I had simply made a mistake.

I continue to learn new things all the time. I'm delighted when a customer comes up to me in the greenhouse and shares a new insight or an ingenious gardening tip. One of my greatest pleasures is trying out a new idea that someone has suggested to me.

If you learn something from me, that's wonderful. But if I'm the only one you listen to, you're missing out on an awful lot. There's a wealth of gardening wisdom out there, some of it as near as your neighbour's back yard.

And don't be afraid to experiment on your own. If something I've said or written doesn't quite fit with your own instincts, for heaven's sake, try doing things your own way! You never know what you might discover—and I'd love to hear your results.

After all, trying new ideas is how I got this knowledge and experience in the first place! ❧

Food for Thought

I BELIEVE VERY STRONGLY in education, so whenever I'm asked to speak at a school, I do my best to come—although I must admit, sometimes I leave my preparations until the last minute.

One warm June morning, I visited a grade five and six class. The only topic I could come up with to talk about was "Watering in the Greenhouse." When I got there and saw how tired the kids looked, my heart sank. "Oh crum," I thought, "they aren't going to listen to a word I say."

Just then, my eye caught a pair of familiar, brightly smiling faces. Two little Italian boys, who often came out to the farm with their parents and grandparents, were sitting in the front row. With a flash of inspiration, I realized I didn't have to talk about watering after all.

"Let me tell you a little story," I said. "Years ago on our farm, we didn't grow very many different kinds of vegetables. We had never grown broccoli or zucchini. Then, one day, some Italian customers came out to our farm and told us how to grow it and even how to cook it. The next year, we planted some. It was wonderful."

The Italian boys sat there, beaming with pride. I began to look around at the other faces and realized that practically every ethnic group was represented in that classroom. So, I carried on with my strategy.

"We had German customers who taught us about growing big cabbages and making sauerkraut. Lebanese folks told us that vegetable marrow was especially delicious when picked small—they called it *kousa*. East Indians introduced us to hot peppers and showed us different ways to cook with them."

I noticed one small boy in the back. I couldn't see him very well without my glasses, so I tried to guess. "The Chinese people told us about using vegetables in stir-fry." The boy didn't bat an eye. "Darn," I thought, "I made a mistake." So I tried again. "And the Japanese showed us *daikon* and the different ways they cook vegetables." Still no reaction. Finally, he put up his hand and asked, "Mrs. Hole, what did the Koreans teach you?" Fortunately, I had recently tried *kim chee*, Korean pickled cabbage, so I talked about that.

By now, the rest of the kids were jumping up and down, their hands waving in the air. "What about the Yugoslavians? What about the Hungarians?" Of course, I didn't have an example to give each and every one of them, so when I was stumped, I simply asked, "What did you have for dinner last night?" When the child answered, I replied, "That's it!" and made a mental note to add those dishes to my vegetable repertoire.

❧❧❧

When I tell this story, I always add a fictional kid who asks me, "What did the English teach you?" I say, "Not much!" My husband, who's of English descent, gets a big kick out of that!

But you know, those kids made me realize something. If it hadn't been for new Canadians introducing us to all kinds of different, wonderful vegetables, our business wouldn't have been nearly as successful. Because we were able to offer so many kinds of produce, people came from miles around to shop at our place.

I like to think of that phenomenon as a reflection of Canada's success. Our diversity is our greatest strength. ✿

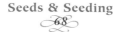

...tasty and nutritious...

Spinach

MY DAUGHTER-IN-LAW VALERIE once remarked that you can throw spinach seed at the ground and get a crop. Well, it's not quite that easy, but it's close. Spinach is also one of the few vegetables that can be grown in light shade, and it tolerates relatively cool weather.

Dealing with bolting

I seed spinach all season long because spinach tends to bolt (go to seed) if there's a stretch of hot weather. When the days start getting longer than twelve-and-a-half hours, the flowering process is initiated and leaf production decreases, replaced by tough, woody stems. With multiple plantings, you can make up for the losses to bolting. The seed is cheap, so why not? The crops from later plantings will probably suffer from a bit of bolting, but in the long run, your harvest will be terrific.

❧ Scientists have recently discovered that spinach (and certain other leafy greens) contains nitroreductase, an enzyme that can neutralize explosive compounds like TNT. The enzyme converts dangerous compounds into simpler, less lethal chemicals, which can then be handled safely.

Popeye Jim

When he was 5 or 6, my son Jim used to carry a can of spinach around in his back pocket, mimicking Popeye, the cartoon character whose exploits he loved. Jim would remove some spinach from the can, gulp it down, and pretend he was super-strong. These antics didn't last long, though: Jim couldn't stand the taste of spinach and had to give up the habit—along with any chance of a career in show business!

Leaf of Choice: Melody

This is the variety you often find in the supermarket. It's easy to clean, tasty, and nutritious—and it's relatively resistant to bolting. Popeye would approve!

Spinach seed germinates quickly. I seed every two weeks until early August for a continuous supply of greens. Each plant will provide a family of 4 sufficient greens for a single meal.

…delightfully different…
Swiss Chard

CRISP AND TASTY SWISS CHARD is more than just an unusual salad green—it can also make a delightful, edible centrepiece! Our florist, Lesleah Horvat, lined a clay pot with Swiss chard, then filled it with a cluster of purple peppers, cherry tomatoes on the stem, curly willow, verbane, and artichoke, to create a medieval-theme arrangement. You could try something similar with colourful vegetables and edible flowers in a crystal bowl.

You can also drop Swiss chard in a stir-fry or use the leaves in place of cabbage for cabbage rolls. This versatile vegetable grows so easily, I always save a spot for it in my garden!

Sifting seed
Swiss chard seeds are odd little things: they look like tiny meteorites with their irregular, deeply grooved surfaces. They're so rough, they can wear through the rubber belts on mechanical seeders in less than a year—this has happened to us more than once.

These seeds are also wonderfully tactile: it's fun to thrust your hands into a pile of them! This is true of all seeds, really. There's a certain fascination to sifting through piles of seeds—it's almost a hypnotic power. In fact, seeds are often used in therapy for people who suffer from neurological disorders involving their sense of touch.

Leaf of Choice: Bright Lights
Bright Lights is really something else. Its roots, stems, and veins are multicoloured and intense; the neon hues make both the garden and the dinner table dynamically different.

Plant Swiss chard in the first week of May. Red chard shouldn't be planted too early, since it has a tendency to bolt if the weather is cool. To harvest, simply run a knife along the row and gather the bundles of clean, soft leaves in your arms.

Radicchio
Another unusual vegetable recently making its debut on North American tables is radicchio, also known as Italian chicory. This leafy vegetable is very visually appealing—perfect for adding brilliant crimson highlights to salads—and is also an excellent source of vitamins A and C.

Radicchio was a trendy vegetable in the 1980s, but it has now caught on with home gardeners and I think it's here to stay. Cooler day temperatures help to sweeten the flavour of this slightly bitter vegetable, so I recommend seeding it in late June or early July. It will be ready for harvest in the first or second week of September.

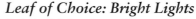

...plant early and often...

Radishes

SINCE RADISHES MATURE SO QUICKLY, they're an ideal candidate for multiple plantings. I know of gardeners who have had 16 plantings in a single season! But we generally seed only 4 times in our garden.

Radishes are prone to going to seed. When exposed to the long, hot days of summer, radishes will bolt like nobody's business. But after asparagus, they are the first vegetable out of the garden. For this reason, I recommend planting early and often to miss the conditions that encourage bolting.

Hot stuff

The flavour of garden radishes can become almost as strong as horseradish. Most of those found in supermarkets are far blander than the ones that we used to grow, mainly because we didn't dilute the flavour with intense watering. The more stress radishes are subjected to, the hotter they will be by harvest time. Many of our customers actually preferred the intense flavour of our hot radishes, though some, used to mild supermarket radishes, found ours too strong for their liking.

Bunches of radishes

We once used the carrot harvester, which chopped off the tops, to harvest radishes, but people seemed to like their radishes sold in bunches with the tops on. I think the days of bunched radishes may be numbered: the labour costs involved in harvesting them this way are very high.

❧ You may want to wear gloves when pulling up radishes. The leaves have coarse hairs that are sharp enough to scratch sensitive skin.

❧ The comic strip we know as "Peanuts"—the one with Charlie Brown and Snoopy—is known as "Radishes" in Denmark.

❧ According to German myth, a certain species of wild radish can be used to identify witches in disguise.

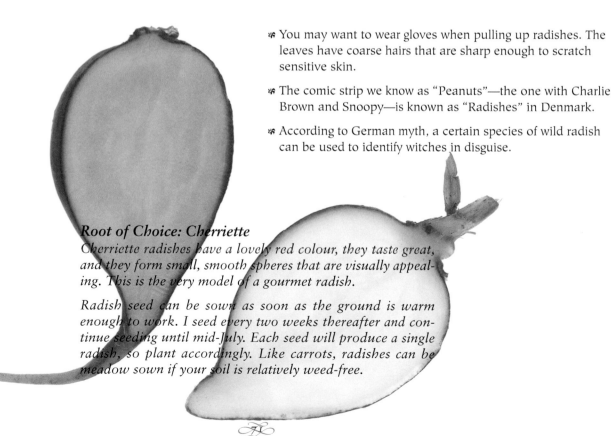

Root of Choice: Cherriette

Cherriette radishes have a lovely red colour, they taste great, and they form small, smooth spheres that are visually appealing. This is the very model of a gourmet radish.

Radish seed can be sown as soon as the ground is warm enough to work. I seed every two weeks thereafter and continue seeding until mid-July. Each seed will produce a single radish, so plant accordingly. Like carrots, radishes can be meadow sown if your soil is relatively weed-free.

When To Plant

I often think that schools should teach risk analysis to young people. A man once came up to me in the greenhouse, a tomato plant in each hand. It was a warm day in May, and he wanted to know if it would be safe to plant them directly into his garden. Safe? I had to chuckle: the tomatoes were on sale for a dollar apiece. I looked him right in the eye and said, "Go ahead—live dangerously! If you win, you win big. If you lose, you lose two bucks!" The man considered this for a moment, smiled, and paid me his two dollars.

We think nothing of plunking down our hard-earned money for a lottery ticket, even if the chances of winning are one in ten million. In our spare time, some of us go skydiving, rock climbing, or even bungee jumping. Yet we wait for the May long weekend before planting a single seed, because we're afraid to take a risk. Get out in your garden in April! Sure, you're taking a chance, but in this lottery you're practically guaranteed to come out ahead.

One sunny day in July, we were out in the field with our boys, weeding. Jim, who was ten years old at the time, turned to his dad and asked, "What day can I have for my summer holidays?"

ञ्चन्चन्च

In farming, good weather is almost always accompanied by hard work. You really do have to make hay while the sun shines, as the saying goes. Since we didn't have much hired help back then, we couldn't afford to waste time. So when we did get a good rain, it was cause for both celebration and relaxation.

While the city folks sat inside lamenting all their spoiled fun, we thought about our thirsty crops. Rain is a make-or-break proposition for farmers. If, as the legend goes, the Inuit have twenty different words for snow, farmers have almost as many names for rain. There's drizzle, soaking rain, pounding rain, and the highly coveted three-day soaker, to name just a few.

Anytime the right kind of rain came at just the right time, Ted would gaze out of the window and say, "That's a million dollar rain." He wasn't just thinking about our place, but about all of the farms in the area.

A good rain was our signal for an impromptu holiday. Since there was no work we could do out there in the muck, we gave ourselves permission to take a break and have fun.

When the boys were young and the first truly rainy morning came along each summer, I'd turn to them and say, "Hey boys, it's your birthday today!" Now Bill's real birthday is in August and Jim's is in early October, both very hectic times on our farm. It's not that they didn't know the truth. As far as they were concerned, though, their birthdays were on the same day. They never asked, "How come you didn't say yesterday that tomorrow was our birthday?" or "Why does it always rain on our birthday?" They just accepted the arrangement.

We'd have an instant party. I'd whip together a cake, and they'd invite their friends from down the road. If my mom and dad had time, they'd come out and join the celebration.

I used the same strategy with the annual Klondike Days festival in Edmonton. If the weather was sunny all that week, we wouldn't get the chance to go to the

Exhibition. However, there was almost always at least one wonderfully rainy day. We'd put on our rubber boots and raincoats, and off we'd go. With practically the entire fairground to ourselves, we'd have an absolute ball.

I remember one rainy afternoon when the boys were quite a bit older. A downpour turned a summer-fallow field into a sea of mud. The boys had a brilliant idea. They called up their football buddies from high school and a whole crowd came over. Out they went, into the field. Although they started out playing an ac-tual game, it quickly dissolved into chaos. The boys were slipping and sliding all over the place, tackling each other and diving face-first to make spectacular catches. I've never heard so much whooping and laughing in all my life. When it was over, we actually had to hose them all down. The "Mud Bowl" remains a neighbourhood legend to this day.

Yes, rainy days certainly provided us with some of our best times and fondest memories on the farm. Maybe that's why I still enjoy splashing through a mud puddle now and then.

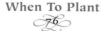

...unglamorous but faithful...

Potatoes

WHEN MY SONS WERE CHILDREN, they used to plant "netted gem" potatoes in a patch of clay soil near the house. The spuds developed a nice, netted skin, sort of like burlap, and they were never knobby: clay soil, which holds moisture, prevented the inconsistent water levels that can lead to those knobs. Clay is tough to work in, but the results certainly make it an option worth considering.

We tend to take the humble potato for granted these days, and what a shame! It's versatile, tasty, and easy to grow, so if you have a bad patch of land where nothing else will grow, fall back on the unglamorous but faithful potato.

Crop rotation

When you grow potatoes, it's important to remember to rotate your crop; that is, don't plant potatoes in the same area of your garden year after year. If you shift the location of your tubers each year, you can avoid disease and insect pests more easily. The Colorado Potato Beetle, for example, will bury itself deep in the earth in the fall and resurface in the spring. It will be looking for potatoes when it emerges, but you can fool it by planting your potatoes elsewhere. The confused bug will wander off, searching for greener pastures. I also try to plant potatoes in a spot where I've grown peas or beans the year before: legumes leave behind rich nitrogen deposits that potatoes love. Practical considerations aside, it's also fun to experiment with the layout of your garden!

Spuds on the lawn

Have you ever driven by a house that had a potato patch instead of a front lawn? Have you ever wondered why anyone would do such a thing? Well, I couldn't blame anyone for wanting a whole yardful of potatoes, but the truth is, planting potatoes is one way to clear out weeds before laying down sod for a more conventional lawn. The foliage shades out many annual weeds, and the constant hoeing kills a good number of the perennial weeds. Some people think this practice will also result in a greener lawn, but harvesting potatoes actually removes nutrients from the soil. But don't worry: you won't damage the potential of your lawn by growing potatoes in your yard, as long as you fertilize.

My favourite potato recipe

It may not sound exciting, but I love to throw potatoes in the oven and bake them. Just thinking about a hot baked potato, one that's fresh out of the garden, makes my mouth water. If I'm feeling adventurous, I'll sprinkle on some dill or fill the skins with onions and chives.

Restaurants use Russet Burbank potatoes for French fries because they absorb less oil—making them less costly to cook. But if you want really delicious fries, use moist potatoes like the Norland variety. They may absorb a little more oil, but the flavour is outstanding.

Don't bother cutting tubers if you want small potatoes. Small, uncut tubers produce lots of small potatoes. The fewer eyes on a seed potato, the fewer tubers will develop—but those that do will be larger than those that develop from a many-eyed seed tuber.

Potatoes love cool nights: they promote tuber growth.

Tuber of Choice: Red Norland

The red-skinned Red Norland is a fairly early-maturing variety, but don't worry—it's known for its long shelf life, so you can grow a large crop and keep them in your basement for use through the winter months. This is the best variety for baking, and the new potatoes taste excellent steamed.

Before planting your seed potatoes, keep them in a warm indoor location (15°C is good) for 2 weeks. Plant the tubers 10 to 14 days before the average date of the last spring frost. Potatoes can tolerate a hard frost after planting, so if the weather is good, take a chance and plant a week earlier still—you'll enjoy an early harvest. A 3 m row will yield about 11 kg of potatoes.

When you're harvesting potatoes, never drop them from a height greater than 15 cm. The potatoes can develop cuts or bruises, which can contribute to disease and decay.

The "Spud Shooter," or potato gun, has been a favourite children's toy for decades.

Believe it or not, researchers have actually developed a mechanical potato. The device gets dropped into a batch of newly harvested potatoes so that its sensors can record the ride through the handling process.

Try "green sprouting" potatoes. If you put seed tubers under fluorescent lights at 8°C for about a month, then plant them as usual, you'll get an earlier crop.

Mrs. Sernowski's Potatoes

ONE YEAR, EARLY IN APRIL, Ted and I were out in the field. We'd had a very warm spring, and it looked as if we would be able to begin planting soon.

Along the riverbank where we live, the land is divided into long, narrow strips, so our neighbours are actually quite close. I noticed Mrs. Sernowski out in her field. I could clearly see what she was doing, although I couldn't quite believe my eyes.

"Ted," I said, "Mrs. Sernowski is over there planting potatoes."

"She's making a big mistake," he replied. "It's way too early. They'll freeze for sure."

"Ted, she's been in the business for 25 years. Maybe she knows something we don't know."

"Nope," said Ted, "they're going to freeze. Mark my words."

I wasn't about to give up. "But Ted," I pointed out, "she's planting three acres!"

Grandma Hole
A Life Well Lived

PEOPLE SOMETIMES MARVEL at my busy schedule and ask me how I find the energy to manage it. I don't think I'm some kind of Superwoman. I pretty much take things as they come and deal with them one at a time. If life starts to get a little crazy, there's no reason to go crazy along with it. Stay calm, keep moving, and you'll always find a way to work things through.

My mother-in-law was a much busier woman than I'll ever be, and I never heard her complain, not once. Grandma Hole knew what it was to work. In an era when child-rearing was largely the job of the mother, she raised nine children—seven boys and two girls—and she was there for each of them. And this was a woman who didn't even have a washing machine until after her fifth child was born!

She always found a way to make every minute of her day count. If a friend dropped by for coffee, Grandma Hole always had her mending bag handy, so she could darn socks while she chatted.

Likewise, she never wasted a single speck of food. She fed nine children on a very limited budget. But nobody cooked a better meal. Nothing fancy, but always very tasty. She prepared the big meal at noon, and in the evening it was always a salad, some cold meat, some nice bread, and lots of tea. She was great at making bread pudding and other puddings with sauces. Those puddings taught me that there's something to be said for English cuisine after all!

From today's perspective, Grandma Hole's life might seem overly traditional and confining. I know she never felt that way, though. She took great pride in running a comfortable, supportive, efficient household. Although she was never involved in her husband's plumbing business, they both recognized the indirect role she played in its success. If she hadn't been able to handle things so well at home, that business wouldn't have stood much of a chance.

She also saw her own success reflected in the lives of her children. She was determined that all of her children would be educated—including her daughters, an attitude not shared by everyone in those days. If she found one of her girls doing housework, she would say, "Don't bother with that. I can do the housework, but I can't do your studying for you."

As a result, all nine of her children graduated from the University of Alberta. At the time, this was an astonishing achievement. The Edmonton Journal published the story, complete with a picture, and that clipping remained a treasured keepsake for the rest of her life.

If I do one thing differently from Grandma Hole, it's that I try to take time to truly relax. I remember her telling me once, "I always felt guilty if I was reading a book, because I thought I should be doing something more productive." If she was reading when her husband came home, she quickly put the book away and got busy doing something else. When she got older and could afford to relax a little, she realized she really didn't know how.

Just the same, she has always remained an inspiration to me. She taught me that by caring for others, and helping them succeed, you can create a truly successful and fulfilling life for yourself. Anytime I feel I'm under too much pressure, or have too much to do, I take a deep breath and ask myself, "How would Grandma Hole have dealt with this?"

Thanks, Grandma Hole. ❧

You Can't Give 'em Away

WE'RE ALL TAUGHT to believe "there's no such thing as a free lunch" and "if it looks too good to be true, it probably is." I generally agree, although every rule has its exceptions. In some people's minds, though, if something's free, there's no way it can be worth anything.

For example: if your household has ever been "blessed" with a litter of pups, you know how hard it is to get "unblessed." It seems as if everyone in the world who wants a dog already has one.

Like most people years ago, we never gave much thought to having our dogs spayed or neutered. As a result, our farm was often visited by the pitter-patter of furry little feet.

It should have been easy enough to find homes for the pups. We kept beautiful purebred German Shepherds. The pups were guaranteed to grow into attractive, gentle, intelligent farm dogs. More often than not, though, our ads or the "Free Puppies" sign we displayed drew little or no response.

But one year, we hit upon the solution. We put a little ad in the paper: "German Shepherd pups. No papers. $10." Inside of two days, they were gone.

It just goes to show: if you literally can't give something away, try selling it instead. ❧

The Dog and the Turkey

SOMETIMES IT'S WISE to keep your mistakes to yourself.

One June, the daughter of one of our close friends was getting married. When there's an occasion like that in a farming community, everybody naturally pitches in. Her family was planning to hold the gift opening on the day after the wedding, and I offered to roast the turkey.

I must say I was pleased with myself when I took it out of the oven. I'd never seen such a glorious-looking bird: it had to be 35 pounds if it was an ounce.

I transported my creation out to the Laurentian, opened the passenger door, and set it onto the floor. As I ran back to the house to grab my purse, the heavenly aroma of the roast turkey wafted through the air.

Apparently I wasn't the only one who thought it smelled good. As I came back out, I saw our dog's backside sticking out the door of the car. And boy, was her tail wagging! When I screamed blue murder, she took off, a drumstick clamped defiantly in her mouth.

I was filled with dread as I ran to the car to assess the damage. My heart sank at the thought of all those guests trying to make do with nothing more than rolls and potato salad. But thankfully, the rest of the bird was untouched.

What else could I do? I carefully sliced away the damaged part, climbed into the car, and drove to the reception. By the time I arrived, I had my story straight. "Ted just loves a leg of turkey," I explained, "and I thought you wouldn't miss it."

Ted has laughed about the story ever since. But do me a favour: if you happen to bump into my neighbours, don't tell on me! ✑

The Tumbler

One Gardener's Secret

THESE DAYS, WE SELL a lot of tomato plants in big five-gallon pails, and almost without exception it's men who buy them. With tomatoes, like many other things, men can be awfully competitive. Whereas a woman spends a dollar or two on a small plant and usually shops for the best-tasting varieties, a man wants big tomatoes and he wants them now. Men love the idea that they can have this big plant in their garden right away and be the first on their block to slice into a ripe tomato.

This trend stretches right back to our very first (and most faithful) five-gallon tomato customer.

Back when the greenhouse was still new, we had planted a half-dozen or so tomato plants very early, just as a trial. This man came out to buy tomatoes for his garden and spotted the five-gallon pails sitting in the back. The plants were thriving, their branches loaded with fruit. Some of the tomatoes were even beginning to ripen.

Well, once he saw those plants, nothing else would do. He had to have one, no matter what he paid.

So we settled on a fair price, and off he went. The next spring he was back, buying his stock of tomato seedlings plus one huge plant. Every year after that, we'd get a phone call from this fellow, asking us to set aside a five-gallon tomato plant for him.

Curiosity gradually began to take hold. I'd hang up the phone and ask my husband, "Ted, what in the world does he do with that big tomato plant every year?"

"Oh," Ted would say, "he probably gives it away as a birthday or anniversary gift."

Finally, one year when the man came out to pick up his order, I asked him, "Why do you always get only one big one? I mean, you must have plenty of tomato plants."

"Oh yeah," he said, "My back yard's full of them."

"Well, is it a gift for someone?"

"I'll tell you, Mrs. Hole," he said slyly. "I take that tomato plant home. I put it in a special place in my garden. And then I call the neighbours over and say, 'See? That's how to grow tomatoes!'"

"You're going to get caught one of these years," I warned him, smiling.

"Oh no," he laughed. "The neighbours keep changing." ❧

Live and Learn

Ninety-nine percent of the things you worry about don't happen; the other one percent you can't do anything about, so why worry at all? That's one of my favourite sayings: it sums up how I feel about life in general, and gardening in particular.

That explains why I'm always telling people to put their gardens in early. Plants like peas, spinach, and lettuce can take a spring frost in stride. Others might represent more of a risk, but most years it's a chance worth taking. The frost will come if it comes; if it does, you can't stop it, and if it doesn't, you have an early crop.

Of course, when disaster does occur, gardeners must be philosophical. No one can predict the weather with absolute accuracy. When it does take a turn for the worse, there's no point taking it personally.

One spring, we planted an entire acre of tomatoes. It had been unseasonably hot the day we put them in—I remember the boys getting sunburns! The plants were growing beautifully. The nights had been warm, the days sunny, and with the end of May approaching, frost seemed out of the question.

As we stepped out the front door one morning, though, the nip in the air was unmistakable. Ted and I immediately ran to check the tomato plants. Sure enough, when we got to the field, we were greeted by row upon row of withered, miserable-looking plants.

Yet the carnage wasn't quite complete. The frost had been strangely selective, killing some plants to ground level while leaving others next to them untouched. Still, we had lost about 85 percent of them.

Of course we were devastated. Our bumper crop had been taken away with one cruel, unexpected blow. By then, even our cautious friends had their gardens planted and like us were shaking their heads in disbelief.

All you can do with an experience like that is try to learn from it. We ended up getting quite a good crop of green tomatoes off the surviving plants, although nowhere near what we had hoped. The plants that had been nipped at the top grew out bushy and wide, and eventually bore some fruit. Even some we thought were completely destroyed somehow grew back from the roots, although, with our short season, they barely had time to flower before fall.

The experience also made us take a long second look at where we were planting our tomatoes. Because they were at the top of a hill, they were far more exposed than they should have been. They lay at the mercy of spring frosts and summer winds.

At the same time, we decided it was time to upgrade our operation. That summer, Ted set to work on a new greenhouse, where the tomatoes were grown from then on, so we would never again have to take that kind of risk with such a large crop of tomatoes. If you plant a half dozen tomatoes in your back yard, you can easily cover them if you're hit by a late frost. If you have a whole acre, however, the bedsheets aren't nearly big enough! I like taking risks, but there's such a thing as being foolhardy.

The most important lesson we learned from those tomatoes, though, was the truth of that old farmers' adage: "There's always next year." Sure enough, we survived to try again. ❧

...in the ground early...

Garland

GARLIC NEEDS A LONG GROWING SEASON: unless it's planted very early, it won't clove. I once told an Edmonton audience on March 21, "It's still not too late to plant your garlic!" I was kidding and many people in the audience laughed, since there's usually still snow on the ground in Edmonton at that time of year. But my friend Mrs. Sernowski always planted her garlic in March, and it's from her example that I plant garlic as soon as the frost leaves the ground—even if it is the first week of March. If the ground freezes again, garlic slips into a kind of suspended animation until the weather warms up. When the heat returns, the bulbs will resume growing. You can also plant in late September for a harvest of large bulbs the following spring.

Clove of Choice: common white garlic

Variety matters less with garlic than with other vegetables, but I recommend planting common white garlic. Elephant garlic produces larger cloves, but it's milder and more difficult to care for than the standard species. Elephant garlic also stores poorly.

PLANT EARLY! If the frost has left the ground in March, get your garlic sets in there! Each set produces one head of garlic, which will contain 6 to 8 cloves—if you like garlic, plant lots! Garlic needs to dry before being put into storage, and the cloves should not be washed or separated.

That distinctive odour

Bill and Valerie once took a trip to Gilroy, California, "Garlic Capital of the World." While they enjoyed their visit, they did note the strong aroma of garlic in the air—which in Gilroy is the sweet smell of success!

On the other hand, Jim likes to tell the story of staff at one greenhouse who once spread ground garlic through the building to disperse bugs. Unfortunately, they used too much garlic and the place became impossible for anyone—staff, customers, or bugs—to enter. On the plus side, it also kept vampires away!

* Never store garlic in the refrigerator: the flavour will be ruined.

* According to Pliny the Elder, the great Roman naturalist, garlic could cure dog bites, bruises and blisters, ulcers, asthma, jaundice, neck swellings, madness, toothaches, ringworm, hoarseness, headaches, coughs, convulsions, leprosy, impotence, and hæmorrhoids.

* In the time of the Pharaohs, it was possible to buy a healthy male slave for about 7 kg of garlic.

...a bit of bite...
Onions

ONIONS REQUIRE A LONG GROWING SEASON—so long that to get the really huge, softball-sized onions, you have to start them indoors and transplant into the garden. We experimented with producing large onions from seedlings for commercial sale, but the high overhead and labour costs convinced us it wasn't profitable. We were forced to go back to seeding onions for the market gardening business.

You can plant onions by seeding them directly into the garden, by transplanting seedlings, or by planting sets. Seeding is the least expensive route, but it's also prone to problems. Transplanting seedlings is a little more expensive and requires the most work, but it gives you a wide selection of varieties. Planting sets is a good option: it's easy, less vulnerable to pests, and the earliest maturing. Sets will also give you those nice, fat onions.

Bulb of Choice: Candy
This brand-new hybrid variety really bowled us over. It tastes just heavenly—sweet and tangy, with a bit of a bite. Best of all, this is a very early variety, with one of the shortest growing seasons for onions I've seen.

I plant either very early in the spring (using seeds, sets, or seedlings) or sow seeds late in the fall for a good crop of big, fat onions. A 3 m row will produce about 18 kg of onions, enough to last most families several months. Store onions in a container that allows for good air circulation, like a wire basket or mesh bag.

Like most vegetables, onions benefit tremendously from early planting. Get onions into the garden as soon as the soil can be worked! Onions can survive temperatures as low as -7°C, so don't let the threat of frost prevent you from planting early.

Care and feeding
How you water onions has a tremendous impact on their development. If the moisture supply is inadequate during the early growth stages, onions will "bulb out": the plants will start producing new bulbs instead of vigorous top growth, resulting in small onions. But never water onions after the first week of August: watering delays maturity, and the onion skins won't set properly.

Bill and Valerie once toured an onion storage facility in Montreal. During the curing process, the onions were stacked from floor to ceiling against a wall of fans. The fans blew hot air over the onions to dry them out, and the resulting smell was overwhelming!

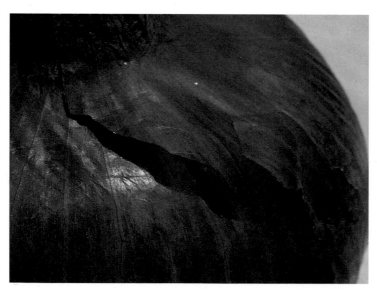

❧ Be careful when hoeing around onions. Onions have a very shallow root system. A careless hoe can injure these roots and reduce bulb size, or cut the developing bulb.

❧ According to old weather lore, "Onion's skin very thin, mild winter's coming in; onion's skin thick and tough, coming winter cold and rough."

...delicious flavour...

Leeks

LEEKS ARE STILL FAIRLY UNCOMMON in my region. They're similar to onions, only they're long and thick instead of short and bulbous, and they can be used for many of the same purposes. I was first introduced to leeks by my friend and former employee, Laura Henry. She started bringing over hot leek and potato soup years ago, and the thought of that rich, creamy broth makes my mouth water to this day. Despite their delicious flavour, leeks aren't very popular here, except with our French-Canadian customers. Perhaps that will change over time; I hope so, because this vegetable really deserves more attention.

❀ To keep the shanks nice and white, mound soil up around the base to block the sun. This will keep them from turning green.

Harvesting tips

Leeks are nearly impossible to pull out of the ground because of their long, heavy, matted roots. I use a shovel and dig them out. Store the harvested plants upright in cardboard boxes, soil and all. If you keep them in a cool location like a garage, you can pull out shanks as needed without worrying about spoilage.

Shank of Choice: Unique

This is an extra-long leek with thick stalks and blue-green leaves. Maturing in mid to late August, it stores well, too.

I transplant large plants into my garden at the beginning of May to produce the biggest, tastiest leeks. A small family will use 1 or 2 leeks per meal; a 3 m row will provide 30 plants.

Transplanting

Have you ever been in a garden centre and seen those long, lanky tomato seedlings that have obviously outgrown their containers? They look so funny, don't they? Sort of like gangly adolescents, with their limbs all over the place. People can be like that too sometimes. Once we put down roots, we get comfortable in our little spaces. We don't want to pick up and try something different—it's so much easier to stay where we are.

But like those overgrown seedlings, we can thrive in a new location, with a new challenge. If we don't transplant from time to time, we stunt ourselves. We need to change to keep growing stronger and better.

Even the tender hothouse seedling must someday face the rigours of the garden. When you get one of those gangly seedlings, you trench plant it. You bury several inches of the stem in the soil, so that the remaining few inches will thrive and become a healthier, sturdier plant. All it needs to succeed is the right change.

preparing dinner, Ted was out in the yard with a bucket, bailing away in the snow. It wasn't exactly his idea of a Merry Christmas.

Finally, at our sons' urging, we agreed to build a new house. It would suit us so much better, they argued—custom-designed from the ground up, with plenty of room and all the latest conveniences. Though my mind agreed, my heart hesitated.

We were talking about leaving the house where Ted and I first lived as husband and wife, where we watched our babies grow into men. When we went into the vegetable business, I greeted customers right there on the lawn. Men, coming off the night shift, would stop for vegetables on their way home, banging on the door at 5:00 a.m. Suddenly, even those memories seemed poignant!

As the weeks went by, and the new house neared completion, I became more and more reluctant. Maybe Bill and Jim should move into the new house, I reasoned. After all, they were grown and needed their own space. The boys were stunned by this suggestion: the change was for Ted and me, they argued, not for them.

Our reluctance to uproot began to tell on us. Although building had started with enormous energy, the finishing details of the new house kept getting put off. The plumbing still

needed connecting and fixtures were yet to be installed. Like me, Ted seemed to be pausing to reconsider the big step.

Our boys sensed that we needed a final push. While Ted and I were out of town at a conference, they shifted most of our possessions to the new house—including our bed! (Jim later recalled that no sooner were we out the door than the truck pulled up to the old house and our belongings started flying!) Unless we wanted to sleep on the floor, we had no choice. The move was made.

While I've grown very comfortable with our "new" place, deep down I still look at that old house as my real home. If you've ever left a house behind after raising a family, you know how I feel.

Our lives are a continuous process of gradual unfolding. Sure, we don't like change all at once, but if we let something grow on us, little by little, we often discover it's not as bad as we imagined. I guess sometimes we all need a little nudge, just to keep us moving and learning. Stability is important, and we need things in our lives that we can rely on, but change is also an important part of living.

If you have strong, healthy roots, you can survive uprooting. You anchor yourself just as firmly in your new location and keep growing.

...tender and sweet...

Lettuce

I ALWAYS SOW LETTUCE SEED VERY THICKLY, because the seed can be sensitive and doesn't germinate consistently. After all, I can always thin later (and eat the tender young plants I remove!).

One year, nearly all the seeds I planted germinated—the crop was absolutely huge! We were thrilled by the rows and rows of new lettuce, anticipating a nice big batch of tender salad greens from the thinning. Imagine our surprise the next day when we found that half the crop had been levelled! A quick investigation revealed the culprit: cutworms. The little pests had gotten to our lettuce before we'd even had a chance to thin it—the cutworms had done the thinning for us. Fortunately, we got rid of the cutworms and saved the other half of the crop. Thanks to thick seeding, we still had a good harvest of lettuce. We were lucky that time—I remember seeing an entire patch of lettuce disappear in less than a week because of cutworms. Remember: one for me, one for the bugs....

Head of Choice: Parris Island Cos

This is a fantastic choice for Caesar salads! Parris Island lettuce is deep green, tastes great, and matures in late July to early August. (Cos is another name for Romaine.)

I like to sow lettuce at least twice each season, once in early May and again in mid-July, after the first crop has been harvested. Don't forget—sow thickly!

Mesclun

Mesclun, a popular new salad vegetable, is actually a mixture of seeds from many different greens. In southern France, it's common to grow all the ingredients for a salad in one pot. Every two or three weeks, when the plants have gained sufficient height, a new salad can be harvested by simply snipping off the greens and tossing them in a bowl. Mesclun is the only vegetable I know that you harvest with scissors!

Our current mesclun mix includes spinach, mustard greens, edible chrysanthemum, coriander, red and green lettuce, radish, spinach, arugula, chervil, and even an edible weed, lamb's-quarters. There are many kinds of mesclun, though; sometimes it's fun to experiment with different combinations of vegetables. Be bold!

❀ Lettuce grows best at temperatures between 16° and 18°C. Germination starts at 4°C, so plant early to avoid the hottest summer days. Properly hardened off lettuce can handle temperatures as low as -7°C. Under hot, rainy conditions, lettuce will get slimy.

❀ To keep leaf lettuce crisp and fresh, wrap it in a tea towel and put it in the crisper drawer of the refrigerator. It will keep for two or three days.

❀ Bitter lettuce results when the plants receive inadequate water and fertilizer; in other words, stress causes bitterness—just as it does in people!

Dig A Little Deeper

I'VE NEVER BEEN QUICK to judge people on appearances. After all, if people judged me on my appearance most days, I'd be in real trouble! It's impossible to work with plants and soil, or at any physical job, and look as if you walked off the cover of a fashion magazine. I'm a farm woman, after all, and I usually look like one.

This can catch some people off guard. Al White, one of our suppliers, still laughs about the first time he came out to our place. He saw this woman out watering the garden, with a dirt-smudged face and windblown hair, soaked with perspiration and the spray from her water hose. "Boy," he thought, "just wait until the boss gets a load of her! She won't last the week!" Of course, that woman was me.

Too many people rely on first impressions. I remember an incident long ago, when I went hunting for boxes to use for packing our vegetables.

Back in those days, banana boxes were the ultimate prize. We sold a lot of lettuce to wholesalers, and banana boxes were absolutely ideal for that purpose. When we stacked the heads in, a dozen per box, they looked just beautiful. If we had to buy similar boxes new, they would probably have cost us 35 or 40 cents apiece. It was much cheaper and easier to find good-quality used ones. Today, of course, wholesalers are much stricter and would not accept boxes recycled in this way. (And yet, old habits die hard: I still find it hard to throw away a good, sturdy cardboard box. In fact, I often joke that when I'm an old woman, I'll spend my time poking around back alleys looking for boxes!)

One morning, I drove to the city, pulled in behind a large grocery store, and, lo and behold, found a veritable treasure trove of banana boxes. I asked a nearby store employee if I could take them. He said, "Oh sure, we're just throwing them out."

So I started to load the boxes up, stacking them very carefully so they wouldn't blow off the truck. All of a sudden, the manager came out. All he saw was this rather disheveled woman, in jeans and rubber boots, stacking up cardboard boxes.

"What are you doing?" he demanded.

"I'm just taking these banana boxes," I replied.

"You've got no business back here," he snarled. "Clear out!"

I drove home, terribly hurt. It had never before occurred to me that people might look down on me simply because of the way I dressed. That man, I decided, needed a lesson in basic courtesy.

I stormed into the house and marched straight upstairs. I got dressed up nicely, put on my best hat, and drove back to the store. I strode in proudly and asked to see the manager.

"What can I do for you, ma'am?" he asked when he came out. I told him who I was and explained, "I was here earlier this morning getting banana boxes and you were very rude. According to the fellow I asked, those boxes were going to be thrown in the garbage. We live on a farm, and we use those boxes for packing lettuce." He had no answer.

"Next time," I said, "maybe you won't be so quick to judge people." From that day on, he was one of the best suppliers of boxes.

Sometimes my own customers make the same mistake that manager made. Over the years, more than a few have complained to me about the personal appearance of some of our workers.

It started back in the 1960s, shortly after the Beatles became popular. A man came up to me, pointed at one of our best employees, and asked, "Why don't you make that kid get a haircut?" I told him that the young man was hard working, well groomed, smart, and pleasant to the customers. The length of his hair didn't matter to me at all.

It's hard to imagine now, but the length of men's hair was a very hot issue back then. Isn't it funny how things change? In any picture I've ever seen of the classical composers, their hair was long. And I'll bet their hair wasn't as neatly brushed as it is in the pictures, either. Of course, those fellows were radicals in their day, too.

Nowadays, if you walk through our greenhouse, you may spot a tattoo here or there, maybe even a pierced nose. You might also see me in my jeans and rubber boots, looking much as I did gathering banana boxes long ago. ❧

Sharing the Land

My family is privileged to live in a gorgeous location overlooking the Sturgeon River valley. People find themselves naturally drawn to the spot, and I'm happy to share it with them.

I've always told my boys, "You must never turn this place into a fortress." We've had to put up a few fences over the years, especially now that the City of St. Albert surrounds us, but we've never had to worry too much about defending our territory. Our land stretches down to the riverbank, so hikers often pass through our property. I think of them as guests, and the vast majority behave that way.

In my experience, if you expect the best of people, you're rarely disappointed. Treat folks with respect, and they tend to return the favour. And, as always, when you do have a problem, keep it in perspective.

In the old days, young people would occasionally drive up into our field, looking for a quiet place to drink a beer or two. We'd walk over to talk to them, and as we approached, we could see them bracing for an angry lecture. "We don't mind you being up here," we'd tell them. "Just don't let things get too wild and take your garbage with you when you leave." We rarely saw a scrap of garbage and had few troubles.

One of our neighbours had a more serious problem with trespassers. He kept a large gasoline drum up in his field, and unknown culprits had been driving their cars up there for nocturnal refueling. He decided to teach them a lesson. He left his sharp-spiked harrows up there in the grass, with the prongs facing up. In the dark, there was no way the thieves would notice it, and two flat tires, or maybe even four, would teach them a lesson, he reasoned.

Did the trap work? Well, yes, but not exactly as he intended. The following spring, he accidentally drove his own tractor over the harrows. After paying for the repairs, he decided simply to move the gasoline barrel to where he could see it from the house. Sure enough, the thefts stopped.

Aggression almost invariably backfires, and what goes around comes around. I truly believe that if you do your best to generate good will, you'll see it reflected in others. ✎

The Innovator

My husband Ted is a terrific sport and always laughs along whenever I haul out one of my old anecdotes. Good thing, too, because he's a central figure in so many of my funny stories.

But Ted has always been a man of great vision, with an inventive and innovative mind. I saw that the very first day we came out to the farm. There we stood, side by side, two kids from the city, while he told me how we were going to make a wonderful life on this little patch of land, with its aging barn and tiny house. He painted the picture so clearly that I could see it myself.

Of course, once we got down to the actual business of farming, that picture was clouded by dozens of day-to-day details. People who grow up on farms absorb so much knowledge that it becomes second nature. Ted and I, on the other hand, had to learn as we went along.

In the long run, Ted turned his lack of experience into his greatest advantage. Farmers are creatures of habit: if they grow up doing things a certain way, it can be next to impossible to convince them to change. Ted, on the other hand, had absolutely no preconceived notions. He constantly questioned our methods and looked for ways to improve them.

When we started market gardening, the industry was in its infancy in central Alberta. Very few people here farmed vegetables, and those who did weren't operating on the scale Ted envisioned. As a result, we had a terrible time finding appropriate equipment. As far as the manufacturers and suppliers were concerned, we might as well have been growing vegetables at the North Pole.

Ted subscribed to dozens of magazines and catalogues from the United States, where the industry was much better established. He'd go through them page by page, looking for new ideas, methods, and tools. After days of research, he chose a John Deere 1020 because, with its adjustable wheel spacing, it was the most suitable for row-crop work. And if he couldn't find the things he needed, he'd adapt the things he had on hand.

Ted relied a lot on our neighbour Len Adams, a talented welder. He would wander down the road to tell Len his latest idea and Len, always the pessimist, would mutter, "Nope, can't be done. It's not gonna work." Ted would ask, "Well, can you at least give it a try?" He'd go back an hour later, and the tool would be built.

After a few years of digging carrots by hand, which is a terrible job, Ted invented a carrot lifter. He had Len weld two grader blades onto a cross-brace, and hitched it to the 1020. As he drove the tractor along a row, the blades loosened the soil on either side. The carrots just popped right out of the ground, ready to gather.

Ted also loved to experiment with new seed varieties. When we first started market gardening, our neighbours told us not to bother trying to grow corn. Ted shopped for the latest hybrids and kept trying different varieties every year. After several years of experimenting, we grew crop after crop of beautiful corn.

Ted also developed a close relationship with the horticulturists at the Brooks Research Centre, at a time when most farmers were skeptical of scientific approaches to farming. From those gentlemen, we learned to try new technologies, many of which we were able to employ successfully.

Of course, not everything Ted tried worked. But when it did, the rewards could be enormous. For instance, if you could find ways to grow an especially early crop, your profits multiplied. Dill cucumbers, which might fetch fifty cents a pound in August, were worth two or three dollars a pound in July. Ted invested a lot of time and effort in his ideas, and it usually paid off for us.

If people poked fun at his unorthodox thinking, Ted never let it bother him. In the late 1960s, I was on the board of the Rural Safety Council. At the time, we were fighting to have roll-bars installed on tractors and to make their use manda-

tory. Ted saw it as an issue of simple common sense: by spending a couple of hundred dollars, he might save his life or that of one of his kids. When the neighbours got a look at Ted's tractor, all fitted out with a roll-bar, canopy, and radio, they were beside themselves. One of them even climbed right up and danced on the canopy. Ted just stood there and watched, not saying a word.

Of course, his foresight has since been proven right, as roll-over protection systems (ROPS) are now legally required on all new tractors. Ted was also an early advocate of hearing protection, another development that has substantially reduced injury on farms in the last few decades. (In fact, Ted swears he lost much of his hearing operating our first potato harvester—hearing protection came a little too late for him.)

But not all of our neighbours made fun of Ted. Other families in the market gardening business began to keep a close eye on him and often followed his example. For years we had people stopping by our house to check out our crops or borrow equipment.

Ted still helps shape our business and his bold spirit continues to be reflected. Customers often tell me how much they look forward to the new plant varieties we offer each year, and our garden centre is always well stocked with ingenious gardening tools.

So when you read one of my anecdotes about Ted, don't forget that behind the laughter stands a most remarkable man. ✆

Good-bye, California!

I ONCE GAVE A TALK in Toronto, and the woman who introduced me joked, "I want everyone to sit up and listen very carefully to Mrs. Hole, because if she can manage to grow things in Alberta, she must truly be an expert on gardening."

Now it's true that Alberta's climate poses some real challenges to a gardener. But it has its advantages too. Some crops—like lettuce, spinach, and asparagus—absolutely love our cool spring nights, while others—like tomatoes, corn, and cucumbers—take advantage of our long, sunny summer days to make the most of our short growing season. And even though a frigid January morning might make us wonder what we're doing here, there's something to be said for the cycle of the seasons. Our long, cold winters make springtime so special.

And, as friends of ours once discovered, even paradise has its drawbacks.

They had moved to California from Edmonton in pursuit of endless sunshine and prosperity. Unfortunately, although they managed to scrape by for several years, luck was not with them. Their situation went from bad to worse, and they decided it was time to come home to Edmonton.

They sold their car to help pay for bus tickets, packed their belongings into boxes, and started the long trip north. As they were cruising along, they spotted a Volkswagen Beetle, crammed with suitcases and boxes, also heading north. As the Beetle pulled ahead of the bus, they saw a hand-lettered sign on the back: "Good-bye California and all your God-damn geraniums!"

Our friends often chuckle about that sign, and say how nice it is to live in a place where geraniums have the good sense to die every winter. Hear, hear! ✺

Planting Seeds

When I was little, my mother didn't force me to work in the garden. She simply made me feel welcome there from a very early age. She gave me my own plants to look after and reserved a small area for me to grow whatever I pleased. Offered a choice between practising the piano and weeding the garden, I chose one just as often as the other. As a result, I never saw gardening as a chore. It was fun.

I took the same approach with my sons. Of course, like all farm kids, Bill and Jim had the chores to do, like grading eggs, feeding the pigs, watering, and weeding the garden. But I always tried to make it at least a little bit fun. They knew that, as long as the work was done in the end, we didn't mind if they chased the geese or played with the dogs while they worked. I never wanted to make their work on our land something to resent.

Every year we give away thousands of Tiny Tim tomato plants to young children who visit the greenhouse on field trips or with their parents. As they carry the seedlings away, gently but trium-phantly, you can tell by the look on their faces that those plants will be pampered and cherished.

Tiny Tims are a great way to transplant a love of gardening into the next generation. The plants don't take up much space, they don't require staking or pruning, and they bear fruit early. With a little bit of weeding and watering, children can nurture their own little crop. They can eat the cherry tomatoes right there in the garden or carry them into the kitchen as a precious addition to Mom or Dad's salad. It's important for kids to learn at an early age that their work is valuable.

Children are natural gardeners. All you have to do is wait for them to show an interest—and believe me, they will. Once they do, just offer them a bit of creative encouragement. By letting them share in your enthusiasm, you'll give them a gift that will last a lifetime.

You'll also gain some delightful gardening companions! ❧

The Pea Bandits

WHEN I WAS A LITTLE GIRL, raiding gardens was simply part of growing up. Although we never took more than a stalk of rhubarb or a carrot, and were always careful not to cause damage, the risk of capture made our young hearts pound.

That's why, as an adult, I've never been worried about kids sneaking into my garden now and then. For heaven's sake, if that's the worst mischief they get into, we should count ourselves lucky. And if nothing else, it's one way to get them to eat their vegetables!

A lot of people aren't as easy-going, unfortunately. One day back in the 1970s, when we were selling u-pick vegetables, a woman came huffing and puffing down to the house. She had spotted a group of little boys raiding the pea patch and had run all the way from the field to report them. She wanted to see these "hooligans" punished.

Now, normally, I would have shrugged it off. But because this customer was so upset by the incident, I felt compelled at least to investigate the situation. I asked my son Bill to drive the truck up to the pea patch and sort things out.

As the truck approached, four little faces dropped suddenly out of sight between the rows. Bill just sat and waited. When the kids finally poked their heads up for a peek, they discovered all six-plus feet of Bill motioning at them to come over to the truck. "Get in," he told them ominously. "My MOTHER wants to talk to you."

The boys climbed reluctantly into the back of the truck, hanging their heads. I'm sure they thought they were in real trouble. I was waiting for them in the yard.

"So, you boys like to pick peas, do you?" I asked them. They nodded their heads sheepishly.

"Well," I said, "it just so happens that we need some help picking peas. Give me your names and addresses, and come back tomorrow at 7:00 a.m."

For the rest of the week, they obediently showed up to pick peas, a couple of hours before lunch and a couple of hours after. On Friday afternoon, Bill brought the boys down to the house, along with all our other farm workers. I started passing out cheques, including one for each of the four boys.

For a moment they just stood there, dumbfounded. They looked down at the cheques and then up at each other, down at the cheques, then up at each other. One of them asked timidly, "You mean, you're actually paying us?"

"Of course I am," I replied. "You've worked hard!"

He cleared his throat. "Mrs. Hole," he said fervently, "you are the nicest person in the world." I had to fight to keep from laughing. It finally dawned on me that those boys had thought they were being punished, and that if they didn't come out to work, I would phone their parents. Instead, they were all going home with money in their pockets, to tell their folks about the job they found.

I've always felt that, in the long run, punishment often does more harm than good. If kids behave in a certain way simply to avoid being punished, they're not learning a darned thing. Kids need to be taught the value of behaving responsibly.

Instead of coming down hard on those boys, and getting them into trouble at home, I gave them a job to do and paid them for it. As a result, they ended up learning a much more valuable lesson.

And I ended up with a pretty good story to tell. ✑

The Spice of Life

EARLY IN MY LIFE as a gardener, I learned the value of trying new varieties. Every year, horticulturists make remarkable advances, and the benefits of their work are as close as the nearest greenhouse. I love being able to sell new, high-yielding tomatoes or the latest supersweet corn.

The trouble is, it's not always that easy. A lot of people just aren't interested in experimenting. They'll try a plant and if it does well for them one year, swear allegiance to it for the rest of their lives. That's a good attitude when it comes to marriage, but gardeners should be willing to play the field! When necessary, I give them special encouragement.

Twenty years ago, we grew a brand-new variety of marigolds, called Jubilee. Crackerjack marigolds ruled the marketplace back then, but Jubilees proved superior in almost every way. They produced bigger, more plentiful, longer-lasting blossoms, and whereas Crackerjacks suffered a "dead" period midway through the season, Jubilees bloomed throughout the summer.

I was so keen on Jubilees that I decided to stop selling Crackerjacks altogether. Then I noticed something: our customers kept insisting on buying Crackerjacks. I could convince some of them that Jubilees were far superior, but with many others, it was no use. The customers would listen politely, then off they'd go down the road to buy Crackerjack marigolds from another greenhouse.

"Ted," I said to my husband, "what in the world are we going to do?" I hated the idea of selling people an inferior plant.

The next time a customer asked me for Crackerjacks, I couldn't help myself. On the spur of the moment, I said, "Here you go," and handed her a flat of Jubilees. After she left, my son Bill objected. "But Mom, that's dishonest!"

"Oh no it isn't," I answered, "not when Jubilee seed is costing me ten times what Crackerjack would."

Later that summer, the same woman came back to the greenhouse. "After I planted my flowers," she said, "I decided I needed

some more marigolds. I bought them from someone else, and you know, their Crackerjacks just weren't as good as yours."

"You bet your life they weren't," I said and confessed my little secret to her. She's been a faithful customer ever since.

ৡৡৡ

People can also be stubborn about their tomatoes. I can't believe the number of people who come in and ask for Bush Beefsteak, even though there are now so many better varieties. Some company dreamed up the name years ago, and now a lot of folks think it's the only kind of large tomato available.

Bush Beefsteak's one advantage is that it's a non-hybrid. If you grow non-hybrid or heritage tomatoes, you're helping to preserve biodiversity. Unlike hybrid tomatoes, it produces seeds that can be successfully grown the next year. However, there are far better non-hybrid tomato varieties out there. The Manitoba, for instance, easily outperforms Bush Beefsteak.

All the same, I'm always after my customers to try a few hybrid tomatoes each year. If they can't be convinced to buy them, sometimes I actually give them a couple, just to try. I might give them a Sugar Snack if they're looking for a cherry tomato, a Northern Exposure if they want a slicing tomato, or a Mama Mia if they ask for a Roma-style paste tomato. Once they see how much fruit these plants produce, and how good they taste, they're hooked.

There's nothing nicer you can do for gardeners than give them something new or different to try. They absolutely love it. They take the plants home, tend them, water them, and then report back with the results. By giving away a few seedlings, we get some marvellous feedback and make a lot of good friends.

So please, experiment with a few new varieties each and every year. And let me know how it grows! ✀

...a perennial delight...

Asparagus

TED AND I HAD ALWAYS HEARD that asparagus was a warm-weather vegetable, so we were a little nervous the first time we planted it. After all, asparagus is one of hot and sunny California's main vegetable crops. Guess what? We found out that it actually grows just as well in our climate. In fact, asparagus is a hardy vegetable that is well suited to Canada and the northern United States. Our biggest obstacle was overcoming our preconceptions about the plant.

Asparagus is a perennial plant, so its placement in your garden is crucial. Remember, it's going to reappear every spring. Years ago, Ted planted asparagus a little too close to the ditch. Over the years, the grass kept encroaching until it became necessary to till the entire field down to black earth. With the tractor, Ted disced 15 cm deep; but to our surprise and delight, the asparagus came back. That was when we realized that asparagus roots are deep

enough to escape the blades. The roots of most grasses and perennial weeds are much shallower; discing allows us to keep the patch weed-free.

Pick a sunny, weed-free location in good, rich soil that's well separated from other perennials. Keeping the asparagus patch weed-free is the key to growing this vegetable, so before you plant, kill as many weeds as you possibly can, especially perennial weeds. You will extend the life of the plants a great deal—with diligence, you can keep them producing for twenty years!

First out of the garden

I always joke that it's easy to tell when asparagus is ready to harvest. I just look out the window and watch for my daughter-in-law Valerie: every spring, she's out in the garden searching for ripe spears. Fortunately, she never has long to wait, because asparagus

is typically the first vegetable in the garden to mature. First out of the garden—and first on the dinner plate!

I don't recommend starting asparagus from seed. You won't be able to harvest any spears for at least three or four years, and unless you're really lucky, fewer than half the seeds you sow will become mature plants. Unless you're really determined and patient, save yourself some time and grief and buy crowns from a garden centre or nursery. My friends sometimes grow asparagus successfully from seed, but they always go back to using crowns. They just can't wait four years to sink their teeth into fresh spears!

Spear length increases when temperatures are high, so expect longer spears during hot spells and shorter ones when the weather is cooler.

* In *Day of the Triffids*, a low-budget science-fiction film from the early 1960s, humanity is menaced by creatures that look suspiciously like giant asparagus spears…

* For some poor souls, asparagus has an unfortunate side effect. After eating asparagus, they discover that their urine emits a rather pungent odour somewhat akin to rotten eggs. This is because these people possess an enzyme that breaks the asparagus down into sulfur-containing compounds.

Harvesting tips
Never harvest asparagus with a knife, as this can spread disease. Instead, gently snap the spears with your fingers; they break easily at exactly the point between tender and woody tissue. Ideally, the spears you're harvesting should be at least 1 cm in diameter and 20 to 25 cm in length. Harvest only as much asparagus as you can eat right away: it doesn't store well. Protect cut spears from the sun and get them into the fridge as soon as you can. Remember that a few spears must be allowed to mature to produce leaves to prepare for next year's growth.

My favourite way to eat asparagus
Here's an easy way to prepare asparagus. Wash enough spears for the family and lay them in a pan. Steam lightly, drain, add lemon and butter to taste, and season with cracked pepper. Serve immediately. What a lovely treat!

Spear of Choice: Jersey Knight
I grow Jersey Knight, a hardy and delicious variety that produces high yields and is resistant to asparagus rust disease.

I prefer to plant two-year-old crowns for a quicker harvest, but if you'd like to start from seed, do it early—in late March or early April. After the first season, expect each plant to yield a half-dozen or more spears. Seven or eight crowns will feed a family of four for several weeks.

...deliciously attractive...

Artichokes

THE FIRST YEAR WE PLANTED ARTICHOKES, we transplanted seedlings into the garden. They seemed to be doing well. But one morning, Valerie discovered they'd been chewed right down to the soil by jackrabbits. We hadn't thought rabbits would go after the seedlings, since at that young stage the plants are rather spiny. The rabbits ate every single transplant, so poor Valerie had to start all over again. The second time around, though, she caged the plants; that fixed the problem.

While artichokes won't get as huge in Canada as they do in California, they're still worth growing. I plant them in good, rich soil in a sunny spot, and they do just fine. We also grow them in pots, where they thrive.

Over-ripeness

As anyone who has grown artichokes knows, you must harvest them when the petals on the globe are still tight. If you cut too late, the flowers will be too close to maturity to eat. The first time we grew artichokes, we let the hearts get a little over-mature. The result was a batch of tough, woody, nearly inedible hearts. Realizing our mistake, we didn't harvest any more. But this was how we discovered that, when dried, the mature hearts make beautiful cut-flowers; we've been using them in dried floral arrangements ever since.

Flower of Choice: Green Globe

These plants produce high yields of thick, flavourful hearts. Green Globe artichokes can reach 1.5 m in height (smaller in cooler climates), so be sure to leave enough space for them in your garden

Artichokes can be transplanted into the garden in late April—these plants can take a hard frost. Expect to harvest anywhere from 3 to 7 globes per plant.

❧ The artichoke is a member of the thistle family. The same species of aphid that attacks Canada thistle also enjoys artichokes, but the pest doesn't usually affect the plant's health.

...tasty tubers...

Sweet Potatoes

You'll never know how good sweet potatoes can taste until you grow your own. This is one of those vegetables that tastes so much better home-grown. Store-bought sweet potatoes just can't compete!

Sweet potatoes love the heat, thriving in the deep southern United States, but they will also grow in Canada, provided they are started in the garden from good-sized transplants. Sweet potatoes are actually one of the easiest vegetables to grow: they're light feeders, they can tolerate acidic soils, and they'll even withstand drought. Keep in mind, though, that while sweet potatoes will grow in cooler areas, the tubers will not get as large as their southern counterparts.

Sweet potato leaves always turn purple immediately after transplanting, but don't panic: it's only because the roots, used to the confines of a pot, take time to spread into the garden soil. Until they get used to the new environment, they can't get at the phosphorus. Soon enough, the leaves will be a nice, healthy green.

Consistent watering is crucial: sweet potatoes will split if the amount of water they get fluctuates widely. Don't subject sweet potatoes to repeated cycles of "drought and soak."

Unwelcome guests

We had a frustrating time raising sweet potatoes one year. Some pesky rabbits managed to destroy two full crops; the third time, we used hot caps to protect the plants. That did the trick, but it was still upsetting to lose so many plants. Pests are part of gardening, and I can't get too upset with the rabbits; after all, they have to eat too. I just wish they'd stay away from *my* garden!

Tuber of Choice: Georgia Jet

This is a good variety for short-season gardens: it has a shorter growing season than other varieties, it reliably produces heavy yields, and it has delicious, moist orange flesh.

Because sweet potatoes are fairly sensitive to frost, I transplant seedlings into the garden around the end of May. Expect to yield about 6 kg of sweet potatoes from 10 plants, enough to provide 6 to 8 meals for a family of 4.

Care & Nurture

Every gardener knows the awesome sense of responsibility our plants create in us. We water. We tend. We chase bugs and add fertilizer. We prune and support the best we can, and we fret and worry—then let nature take its course.

Our gardens are expressions of ourselves. We put our best into our gardens—we care about them and want them to thrive. We want to brag about our tomatoes and zucchinis, our bumper crops and patient accomplishments. Caring is the soul of gardening.

Life is that way too. With our families, our work, even our hobbies, we do our best, but can only do so much. We take risks and place our trust in factors beyond our control. Yet in the end, we are almost always rewarded with a beautiful harvest.

Crops continue to grow, even when you're living through a difficult period. You may be suffering terribly, but the demands of farm life don't disappear. Even during the toughest times, farmers have to find a way to get up in the morning, face the day, and get their work done.

This can feel unbearably harsh. But, as I discovered early on, in some ways it can also be a blessing and a comfort.

Ted and I were expecting our first child, and like all prospective parents, we had gone through months of exhilaration and anticipation. A few weeks before the due date, however, the doctor discovered that something had gone terribly wrong. When I went to the hospital to deliver the baby, my heart was heavy with anxiety and dread.

To our immense sorrow, our child, a daughter, lived only three short days after she was born. I remained in hospital with a serious infection. "Many people survive worse experiences than this," I reminded myself over and over. Even so, the bright July sunlight streaming through the window seemed like a cruel, personal insult.

That same sun, however, was also shining on our farm. The weather had been particularly fine that summer, and although it was early in July, we already had a whole field of early potatoes ready for sale. Despite his grief, Ted was trying to run the farm on his own. He had some help to harvest the potatoes, but he couldn't possibly find time to arrange to sell them as well.

There was no way around it. Our income depended on the sale of that crop. I had a phone brought into my room and called the wholesalers from my hospital bed. Each time I dialed the phone and talked to someone, a little of my strength returned. By the end of the day, I had sold the entire crop, and I realized how much better I felt. In the midst of our sadness, Ted and I kept working together toward a common future.

It also helped to know that we could depend on the support of our neighbours. When my good friend Mrs. Gervais heard that I was going into the hospital, she said, "You send Ted over here for his meals."

"Oh, that would be wonderful," I told her, "but I want you to let us pay you for them." Reluctantly, she agreed to accept 50 cents.

Well, for that 50 cents, Ted got more food than he knew what to do with. He went over there every day for the big noon meal, complete with potatoes, home-made bread, and a marvellous dessert. He'd report to me in the hospital about the delicious pies Mrs. Gervais made. The Gervais family treated him like a king.

Those meals not only made things easier, but they made Ted feel better. At times like that, people often neglect to eat properly, and the situation becomes much harder to bear. Our neighbours saw to it that Ted had plenty of healthy food and good company. They also made sure I had one less worry.

Life, of course, did go on. I still carry some of the pain of that early loss, but feel blessed that I had my husband, my friends, and my farm to help me endure it.

...greens and all...

Beets

TIMING IS EVERYTHING IN GARDENING. Planting too early or too late can have disastrous—or at least annoying—consequences. Beets, among the earliest vegetables you can seed, taught me the value of knowing when to plant.

Detroit Dark Red was the standard beet when we were starting out. Compared to today's varieties, it left something to be desired. For one thing, it could be pithy and woody; for another, it had a tendency to bolt (go to seed). To combat this, we reasoned, we would plant lots of beets very early and avoid the long days of summer that cause bolting. It worked, all right, but we wound up having far too many beets too early in the season, when we couldn't get rid of them all, and only huge beets by mid-season. That was when we decided to do multiple plantings. Newer varieties like Pacemaker and Red Ace, resistant to bolting, also helped to eliminate the problem.

So appealing

Bright-red beets are a terrific addition to the dinner plate, adding colour to the bland hues of meat and potatoes. There's another way to enjoy beets, though, and that's to harvest the greens. Ted and I prefer beet greens to spinach: they're delicious! We actually grow beets specifically to harvest the leaves. I pick them when the plants are fairly young and the leaves are about 10 to 15 cm tall; the tender young roots are a nice bonus.

Too many beets

Our greenhouse manager, Dave Grice, recalls having to "top" (remove the leaves) long, large trailer-loads of beets stacked several feet high. After a while, his hands would be stiff and—naturally—beet-red. He really loved the vegetable, though, and ate cooked beets like candy. Dave nearly fainted one day when he saw that his urine was bright red. Thinking himself gravely ill, he was relieved to learn that it was merely discolouration due to eating too many beets. Despite all of this, Dave still loves beets!

Blackheart

From time to time, we would notice a black spot in the heart of our beets. It's called "blackheart" and is caused by boron deficiency in the soil. Boron is the chemical responsible for sugar storage; it's required by all vegetables, usually in trace amounts. Beets and cauliflower require more boron than other vegetables. If you find that blackheart is a problem, micro-nutrient supplements that can be added to the soil are available .

Root of Choice: Pacemaker III

Pacemakers are great-tasting, tender, solid-red beets. You can begin harvesting when they reach the size of a golf ball, and they don't become tough or woody when they get larger. Enjoy them greens and all!

I seed beets at least twice in a season, first in late April (providing the ground can be worked), and again two weeks later. A 3 m row will produce 4.5 kg of beets, plus several meals of tender young beet-tops.

❀ Leave some stem on the beet when you harvest. If you cut too close to the vegetable, beets will bleed (that is, lose much of their colour) when cooked.

The Beet Incident

IF YOU WERE TO ASK me the one time I was angriest at my husband, I wouldn't have to think for a second. I have never, ever been more furious at Ted than I was the day he ploughed under an entire patch of beets.

When I say it that way, it sounds ridiculous. Who would get so upset over a few beets? Well, let me tell you, to this day I can't even think about it without getting a little bit hot under the collar. Vegetable farming was such a struggle that to plough under any vegetables struck me as a horrible act.

To be fair, I have to say that they were pretty pathetic beets. It had been a dry summer, and they hadn't received nearly enough water or attention. Unless you looked closely, it was difficult even to spot the beet greens among the weeds.

Still, they were the only beets we had. I knew that in a few weeks people would start asking for beets, and it would be nice to have at least something to offer them. So one morning, I asked Mrs. Durocher to weed the beet patch. I watched her work for a few minutes, moving through the rows slowly and meticulously as only she could, and knew the crop could be salvaged. I headed off to a School Board meeting feeling greatly relieved.

When I returned, around suppertime, I went up to see how Mrs. Durocher had managed. I stood at the edge of the field, my mouth agape. The entire patch was demolished. There was nothing there but freshly turned soil.

Apparently, Ted had also noticed how badly the beets were doing. Without asking me, he had decided they were more trouble than they were worth and went out to plough them under. When he got to the field, he hadn't even noticed that the beets were newly weeded. He just went ahead and destroyed the crop.

I was livid. What on earth would I say to Mrs. Durocher when she arrived for work the next morning? All that effort wasted without a moment's thought! I suspected her feelings would be hurt, yet she never said a word. She must have trusted that we had a good reason for changing our minds.

Of course, we didn't.

Ted should have consulted me before making that kind of decision. After all, I was the one who dealt with the customers, and I was the one who would have to spend the rest of the summer apologizing because we didn't have any beets.

That evening, we had friends over for supper and the atmosphere was less than convivial. Much later, they told me, "Lois, we had no idea you could be as angry as you were that night."

Of course, our relationship was solid enough to withstand the bitter experience. It made me understand, though, how marriages sometimes break up over the most trivial things.

It also reinforced, for both of us, the importance of communication and trust, because these problems would always happen. We couldn't afford to assume that we each knew what the other was thinking and we needed to know that we could get past our problems.

And finally, it taught me that other people could be much more forgiving than I. ❧

The Family Boat

WHEN PEOPLE CAST A nostalgic eye back, their minds often drift to warm memories of the family car. When I think back to the cars we've owned, though, I don't get all misty-eyed. For decades, Ted and I never bought a new car—we always had second-hand vehicles from relatives. As a result, cars weren't that special to us. Nonetheless, some of our best family anecdotes revolve around cars.

One frosty November day, years ago, we were driving down Kingsway Avenue in Edmonton when for some reason our trunk suddenly popped open. We turned right onto 109 Street and came to a red light, so Ted got out of the car to close the lid. He leaned over, slammed the trunk lid—and caught his tie in it.

I was sitting in the front seat with the radio turned up, waiting. Then in a quiet passage, I heard a lot of thumping and banging. I turned around and couldn't even see Ted's head. All I saw was his hand, pounding furiously on the trunk.

By this time the light had turned green, and cars were backed up behind us. I tried to stretch across to find the trunk release lever, but the car had bucket seats and I couldn't reach it. I had to get out of the car, run around to the driver's side, and pull the catch. By this time, Ted was absolutely livid. Cars were tooting their horns, and drivers were laughing as they drove by. Once Ted got back into the car and settled down, of course, he was able to laugh too. It must have been quite a sight!

Despite the beating it took from Ted, the car survived intact. One of our other cars wasn't as lucky.

Back in the early '70s, Ted bought a massive second-hand Lincoln from his brother Jim. This beast was so unbelievably huge and heavy that we called it the Queen Mary. You can imagine the kind of mileage it got. Instead of miles per gallon, we measured it in gallons per mile!

Some people would consider the car luxurious, but it wasn't really our style. I was never completely comfortable driving it. If you've ever been behind the wheel of a car that big, you know how easy it is to lose track of your speed. I got pulled over by the police one day in a school zone, and while I wasn't going that fast, I was certainly well over the limit. I was doubly mortified, because I was a school trustee at the time.

I got out of the car, and the policeman slammed the door shut behind me—locking my keys in the car. I know he was embarrassed by the blunder, but he hid it well. "Next time," he told me sternly, "keep an eye open for the school zones!" Then he got into his cruiser and drove off, leaving me to sort out the problem of my locked car.

The end came when we took the Lincoln in to René Parenteau's garage for minor repairs. One of the young men at the garage didn't realize the mechanics had removed the carburetor and tried to start the car. When it didn't start, he pumped the gas pedal, showering the engine with gasoline. The engine burst into flames, which quickly spread. Nobody was hurt, thankfully, but the car was completely gutted.

Poor René! It took him almost a full day to work up the courage to phone. The next day, around noon, our son Jim got the call. René apologized again and again. I think he was desperately worried about what we would say.

Jim approached his father and cautiously broke the news to him. He expected Ted to be upset, but instead, his dad burst into gales of laughter. "Never did like that stupid car anyway," he chuckled.

The car carried a bit of insurance, so we wrote it off and collected what we could. My only regret is that we were never able to give the Queen Mary a proper burial at sea. ❧

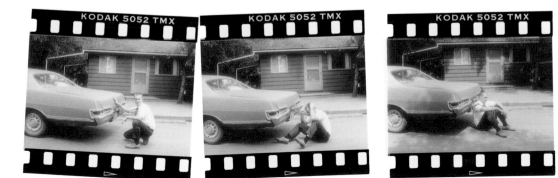

The Most Important Job

I'VE ALWAYS SAID that in a greenhouse or garden, watering is the most important job. To a plant, water is everything. If you water it too much, too little, or inconsistently, you'll have real problems. You'd better do it right.

In the beginning, I did most of the watering myself. Later, as the job became too big for me to handle alone, I always made sure that I had confidence in the people helping me.

People have this strange idea that just because a job appears menial, it doesn't require any brains. In my experience, though, intelligence can express itself in almost any task. We used to hire teachers during the summer to help thin and weed the crops. I'd explain the basic principles once, and they'd grasp them right away. After a couple of days, you'd swear they'd grown up on the farm.

Watering is much the same. Anybody can point the business end of a hose, but it takes real skill to do the job right. I have employees who can look along a row of flowers, sense the temperature and humidity, and know just how much water the plants need. They can tell at a glance when a plant needs moisture, long before it actually begins to wilt.

I was once at a bedding-plant conference and had signed up for a special luncheon. The keynote speaker was Nancy Austin, who had co-written the motivational bestseller *In Search of Excellence*. She told us that as greenhouse managers, we should ensure we put our time to its most productive use. "You people shouldn't be out there watering. That's the kind of job anybody can do. You've got better ways to spend your time."

At the end of her talk, she asked if there were any questions. I just couldn't stand it any longer. I put my hand up and said, "I'm afraid I have to make a small criticism. You may be an expert on time management, but I'm afraid you don't know a lot about greenhouses or plants. You made it sound as if watering were a menial job, one that doesn't take any skill. That's just not true. Watering is the most important job in the greenhouse." Well, the audience practically gave me a standing ovation. They knew that it needed to be said.

I'm surprised at how often I have to set people straight on this issue. I remember a friend of mine who called me one afternoon with an extra ticket for a theatre matinee. I said, "Oh crum, I can't go. I have all this watering to do." She said, "Why don't I get Susan to come out and do it for you?" Susan was her twelve-year-old daughter!

If your plants aren't properly watered, they simply won't thrive. They'll grow unevenly, they won't produce very good blooms or fruit, or they could very well die altogether.

In fact, some plants die before they even break the surface of the soil. People put seeds into dry earth, sprinkle on a little bit of water, and wait. The seeds germinate, dry out, and die. A few times each year, somebody will tell me, "I planted a whole patch of carrots, and not a single one came up." In almost every case, poor watering is the reason.

For goodness' sake, plant your seeds early in the season, while the ground's still moist, then hope for rain. If it doesn't rain, you're going to have to get out there and water thoroughly, every single day.

In fact, that may mean watering even after a rain. Unless you're hit with a real soaker, the rain won't penetrate more than an inch or so beneath the surface. If you just leave it at that, the rain actually causes more harm than good. The roots will grow where the moisture is: near the surface. Without deep roots, your plants will be much more vulnerable to drought later.

Water regularly and water thoroughly. Nothing is more essential to growing a beautiful garden. And if you drop by our greenhouse one of these days, don't be surprised if I'm busy watering. ❧

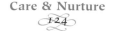

Bill and Jim

I MAY NOT BE THE world's leading authority on motherhood, but when I look at my two grown sons, I feel comfortable in saying I did a pretty good job. Although I made my share of mistakes over the years, Bill and Jim turned out just fine. In addition to being my children, they are two of my closest and most trusted friends.

Being a parent is the most important, most fulfilling, and at times most demanding job in the world. I believe that the bond between a parent and child must, like any successful relationship, be built on trust and acceptance.

I've always made it a point to listen to my children, long before they could talk. When I first became a mother, people believed you should never pick up a baby just because he or she was crying. To this day, some people believe it will spoil the child. I always felt that if my baby was crying, he was trying to tell me something. I can't imagine that children cry for no reason at all.

As the boys grew older, I tried to give them room to make their own choices, rather than tying them down with rules. Of course I provided some boundaries for their own safety, but by and large I trusted them to use their common sense. I simply told them how I hoped they'd act, reminded them to be careful, and let them go their own way. Freedom breeds responsibility, and my sons rarely disappointed me.

Of course, we had the advantage of living on the farm. When they were young, Bill and Jim came home from school on the bus and never really asked to go anywhere else, so they didn't have much opportunity to get into serious trouble. And like most farm kids, they had their chores to keep them busy.

Along with the work, though, came some opportunities that most city kids would envy. When the boys were nine and ten years old, we had this old car, a '52 Chev hardtop. Our truck had become our most important means of transportation, so we let the boys have the car to drive on the farm.

While Ted and I worked, they would carefully drive around in the field. Even though the field was perfectly flat, and they never went very fast, it was still quite a thrill. All their cousins, who regularly went on holidays to places like Disneyland and Hawaii, thought Bill and Jim were the luckiest boys in the world: they owned their own car!

When they were teenagers, we never set any curfews. Again, we trusted them to use their heads. I told them, "You can phone me at any time, no matter where you are, and I'll come and get you." When you make a pledge like that, you really have to mean it. A lot of parents say that, then get mad when their kid phones them after a night of drinking.

The funny thing is that Bill and Jim never had to take me up on my offer. They always came home safe and sound.

Of course, no amount of trust can completely ease a parent's anxiety. I remember one evening, when Jim was sixteen or so, he went out to a party with his pal Larry Kozachuk. Around 11:00, just before I went to bed, Jim phoned to say that he wasn't going to be home for a while. Well, around five in the morning, I woke up for some reason. I went down to Jim's room, and he wasn't in his bed. I felt sick.

My head spun with visions of the boys trapped inside an overturned car or asphyxiated in the garage. I threw a coat on over my nightgown and slipped on a pair of runners. I hurried down the road, examining both sides of the ditch, and peeked into Kozachuks' garage. I didn't find a thing, so I turned around and went home to bed. I thought, "Well, I've done what I can do." A few minutes later, I heard Jim come in quietly through the front door.

I resisted the temptation to rush down and demand an explanation. Time passes so quickly when you're having fun, and Jim has always been a real social animal. He was safe, and that was all I needed to know.

The boys were also lucky to have a reasonable father. Ted made sure that they never had to give up any school function for chores. If there was a football or hockey game, he felt they should be able to take part. They should have time to be kids.

Ted also made allowances for their individual differences, instead of expecting them to behave uniformly. During hockey season, Bill was always ready to go to early morning practices before his little brother got out of bed. Ted would drive Bill to the rink, drive home, then turn right around for a return trip with Jim. And he never complained.

Maybe it's different for parents nowadays. The world has changed so much, and kids are under such intense pressures—particularly in the big cities. Even so, I firmly believe that you have to offer your children as much freedom and trust as you can. In the long run, they'll reward you. ❧

Time For Lunch?

PEOPLE OFTEN ASK ME how we can be in business as a family and still get along. After all, some families have a hard time getting through a holiday dinner without a fight.

I jokingly tell them that it's all thanks to me. If a father and sons are going to work together, they need to have the mother involved as well—to make sure they don't kill each other!

In fact, I think the answer can be found around my kitchen table. It's funny how something so basic can be so much more important than it seems. Over the years, that kitchen table has been our lifeline.

Every day at noon, we leave the office and greenhouse behind and head over to the house for lunch. We catch up with what everybody's doing, chat about the day's events, and subject one another to good-natured ribbing. Although our lunches occasionally include a bit of yelling, and even a tear or two, you're much more likely to hear laughter and friendly conversation.

Lunchtime also gives us a chance to settle our differences, because problems aren't left to simmer day after day. They get worked out right away, and when this happens over a pleasant meal, things rarely get out of hand—even when the family is divided on an issue.

Early in my married life, I learned that if I wanted to raise a difficult topic with Ted, it helped to feed him first. To this day, I don't talk to him seriously until he has something in his stomach. That rule continues to serve me well with my entire family.

When Bill finished university, he had to make a choice about what he wanted to do: join the family business or pursue something else. Naturally, he brought up the difficult topic at the dinner table. He would happily stay on the farm, he said, but only if we expanded our operation significantly. While Ted agreed in principle, he was anxious that Bill wanted to move too far, too fast. Tempers flared, and Ted wound up stomping out of the kitchen.

Despite the fact that Ted was eager for Bill to stay, he was reluctant to relinquish some of his control over the business. When family roles change, the adjustment can be traumatic. A few days later, Ted and Bill sorted out the situation over the kitchen table.

❧❧❧

The kitchen at lunchtime is also our informal boardroom, the one place where everyone knows it's okay to express their opinions. They also know they won't be distracted by customers, phone calls, and the like. The table brings focus to anything that needs debating—or good stories that need sharing.

With the number of strong personalities involved in our business, the work day invariably generates some significant differences of opinion. Just when the discussion threatens to become an out-and-out battle, though, it's time for lunch. Everyone files into the house and eats as though nothing had happened, at least for a few bites. When the problems of the day finally arise, they somehow seem much easier to sort out. Everyone goes back to work with no grudges and no bad feelings.

We often draw other people into the circle as well. One of our suppliers might make a delivery just before lunchtime, or somebody from out of town might be inspecting our trial garden. Dave Grice, a long-time employee and friend, eats with us regularly. When you bring people to your table and feed them good food, you build a bond.

So that's my secret to ensuring harmony. In any business, and a family business in particular, communication is absolutely crucial. And if good food is involved, so much the better. ❧

...up bright and early...

Broccoli

FOR THE FRESHEST broccoli, I get up bright and early and pick before the plants have been warmed by the sun. Broccoli can be harvested at any size; the small ones make particularly tender salad greens. To harvest over a longer period of time, cut the central head when it's still hard and green, along with 7.5 to 10 cm of stem. This encourages the plant to develop side shoots, which you can come back and harvest later.

If the weather is warm, I harvest more often to avoid having buds go to flower. Sometimes we picked too late and wound up having the broccoli flowering on our retail tables! It made a nice display, but few people bought them.

Broccoli is extremely sensitive to post-harvest deterioration, and plants must be plunged immediately into an icewater bath to remove field-heat. Otherwise, the broccoli won't keep long at all—it will become yellow and smelly.

Blankets and broccoli

I've always wondered how my Italian customers used all the broccoli they harvested during our u-pick years. Whole families would arrive—parents, children, uncles, aunts, cousins, grandparents...it was a real family outing. What I found most interesting was the way they harvested broccoli. They would load up blankets with vegetables. When they'd filled up the blankets, they'd get more blankets out of the car, load them up, and wrap them into balls. Some of the women carried off the last of the harvest in their aprons. They would cut everything, even the small broccoli. I admired their enthusiasm, but to this day I still wonder...what *did* they do with those hundreds of pounds of broccoli?

Head of Choice: Small Miracle

Small Miracle gets its name from its large, dense heads that form on very compact plants. Raw or cooked, this variety does miraculous things to your taste buds; it's slightly sweet and very tender.

I seed a number of times, from April to June. If April seems early, don't worry: broccoli can take a light frost. Each plant will produce about 700 g of broccoli.

...succulent white flesh...

Cauliflower

THERE ARE SOMETIMES DISADVANTAGES to growing and preparing your own vegetables. Some years ago, the family sat down to eat dinner, which included cauliflower in a rich, creamy cheese sauce. It smelled wonderful and everyone was about to start eating when Valerie found a cabbage worm in her cheese sauce. Worms occasionally hide in the cauliflower's many nooks and crannies; we'd obviously missed this one when we were washing the vegetables. It had been cooked in the sauce and was perfectly intact, bright green and rubbery. Bill and Jim made fun of Valerie's concerns—after all, it was just one little worm. "Just pick it out, it won't hurt you," Bill told her. Ted was amused: "Go ahead and eat it, it's good for you. More protein." While Valerie excused herself to dump her cauliflower in the garbage, the rest of us continued to eat. However, it wasn't long before we discovered that Valerie's worm was not the only one swimming in the cheese sauce, and soon a heap of infested cauliflower lay piled at the centre of the table. To this day, Valerie won't eat cauliflower without inspecting it very carefully first.

Tender loving care

The succulent white flesh of the cauliflower is a fragile thing. To bring it to fullness, this plant requires the utmost care and attention. Preventing yellow

Head of Choice: Minuteman

I love this early variety! It's ready for harvest in August, the succulent heads get up to 1 kg, and it has good leaf cover to protect the curds from yellowing. Minuteman is a self-wrapping variety.

Transplant cauliflower seedlings at the beginning of May—like broccoli, cauliflower can withstand a light frost. Each plant typically yields about 1 kg of cauliflower, enough for 1 or 2 side-dishes for a family of 4.

heads is a simple, if time-consuming, matter. Once the heads have formed, take some rubber bands or string and fasten the leaves shut over them. This protects the curds from the sun, preventing yellowing. However, the cauliflower plants must be checked daily to see if they have reached maturity. There's nothing wrong with yellow curds, really: they taste a little stronger, but they are by no means inedible. I often pickle cauliflower if it turns yellow, a much better solution than throwing away the curds.

Many cauliflower varieties are self-wrapping—that is, the leaves form a protective layer over the head. The curds of these varieties stay tight and white, making them your best choice for the garden. Cauliflower curds that don't self-wrap are also vulnerable to becoming ricey, a condition where the curd turns rough and begins to develop little seed heads.

Buttoning

Buttoning, or premature curd formation, occurs when vegetative growth is checked, usually when the plant is in a pack. Once a curd starts, nothing can be done; these overgrown, weak plants must not be transplanted into the garden. Buttoning may be caused by a number of factors: too-rapid hardening off, unbalanced fertility, low soil moisture, extreme and continued cold (4°C for 10 days or more), or overgrown pack plants.

Keep it cool

Cauliflower, like corn, has a high respiration rate. The curds will deteriorate rapidly if cauliflower isn't cooled immediately after harvest. We usually put cauliflower in an ice bath as soon as we cut it to keep it fresh.

❧ "Cauliflower is nothing but cabbage with a college education."
—Mark Twain, *Pudd'nhead Wilson's Calendar*, 1893

Harvest Season

Harvest is a time of plenty, when we enjoy the fullness of our efforts. More than any other, perhaps, it is the season of the mind... a time of endings and beginnings, of mingled sadness and celebration.

The end of the growing season is a time for taking stock, for savouring what we've accomplished and enjoying the rewards of our labour. It is also a time for looking ahead. We review what the last season has taught us, then eagerly start planning what we'll try next.

We keep finding ways to enjoy gardening. And we go on, in the cycle of the garden, to begin again, renewed and enriched by a bountiful harvest.

They say that smell can bring back memories more strongly than any other sense, and I'm inclined to agree. Many times I've been stopped in my tracks by a familiar scent wafting past my nose, disoriented for a moment by a feeling of being drawn backward in time. For just an instant, it's like revisiting the past. It's an unsettling, though not unpleasant, phenomenon—one I've experienced many times and often witnessed in others. I'm especially struck by how the smell and taste of a fresh vegetable harvest can bring out people's most vivid memories—you can see it in their eyes and in their smiles. Whenever I see this happen, I remember a particular harvest, more than forty years ago.

Ted's father, Harry—we called him Grandpa Hole after Bill was born—was a plumbing contractor—a tough, no-nonsense man. But he had many other characteristics. He was an unrepentant practical joker, with a deeply introspective side that revealed itself only rarely. During the winter of 1954, he became desperately ill, his trademark vitality sapped by disease. One morning, late in the spring, my mother-in-law called to say she was planning to cook a piece of lamb, his favourite meal. Even though it was awfully early in the season, she hoped I might be able to find some fresh peas, because they were his favourite vegetable.

That, I think, was the signal that the end was approaching, the admission that Grandpa Hole's last days had arrived. I told Grandma Hole that I would do my best. I pulled on a sweater, picked up a basket, and went out to look.

It was a cool, misty morning, with the tiniest bit of drizzle. The moment I left the house, the scents of the garden began to draw me back to the times when Grandpa Hole would come out to visit the farm. He would wander out into the fields, alone, find a spot, and just stand there, becoming part of the landscape. He'd put his hands on his hips and inhale the fresh, clean air, reveling in the innocent atmosphere of the land, not worrying about his business or anything else. As I entered the garden, I could almost see him there, standing in the field wearing his favourite suit, bathed in orange and yellow light as the sun peeked over the horizon.

I checked the first vine I found and caught a glimpse of several pods glistening with dew, barely ready to be picked. I opened one of the pods for a sample and popped a few peas into my mouth. To this day I remember how those peas tasted—fresh and cold, sweet and juicy. The garden was lush with peas, and I realized it was giving me an extraordinary, priceless gift.

Ted's dad got his dinner, roast lamb with fresh peas and mint sauce. He ate every bite, exclaiming what a treat it was to have a home-cooked meal, complete with garden vegetables. In his eyes I could see the memories of happier days. I like to imagine he was thinking about those quiet times in our field, enjoying being one with the land.

Three weeks later, he died peacefully.

Compared with everything Grandpa Hole did for me and my family, that meal seems like such a tiny gesture. I think, though, that he truly appreciated the memories that the taste and smell of those vegetables brought back. I know I will never cherish another harvest as much as I did that basket of peas, and I know that whenever I want to revisit days past, all I need to do is walk in my garden.

…hotter and hotter…

Peppers

TEN YEARS AGO, WE SOLD ONLY green bell peppers. Today, we sell a wide variety of hot and sweet, yellow and red, green and orange peppers—and people keep clamouring for them. It's pretty clear that immigration has influenced Canadian diets, introducing us to all sorts of new culinary delights. What a wonderful way to cross cultural barriers! After all, everyone needs to eat, and discovering new tastes makes life a little livelier.

Perfect peppers

Peppers must be transplanted if they're to have any hope of bearing fruit in areas with short growing seasons. We start them in the greenhouse, move them into containers, and transplant them into the garden in early June, after all danger of frost has passed. One rule of thumb: the cooler and shorter the growing season, the larger the transplants should be before you put them in the garden.

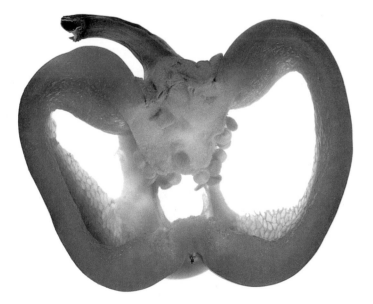

Peppers love warmth and must be hardened off gradually before transplanting. A well-hardened off plant will be short and stocky, not tall, skinny, or floppy. Look for sturdy stems and foliage.

The old switcheroo

When my son Jim was a little younger, he liked to play practical jokes on unsuspecting friends. Once, he took a friend out to the garden to show him some of the ripe peppers. Jim took two peppers in hand—one sweet, one very hot, but both identical in shape and colour. To show how good the peppers were, Jim popped the sweet one into his mouth and made enthusiastic noises. "Mmmm, this is great," he told his friend. "There's nothing like a garden-fresh sweet pepper. Try one." Jim handed his friend the hot pepper, with predictable results. The poor fellow bit into the fruit and immediately started gasping and coughing, tears running down his cheeks. Jim also had tears running down his cheeks—tears of laughter! I'm not sure where he got his sense of humour….

Fruit of Choice: Northstar

Northstar peppers are medium-sized green bells that perform well under cool conditions—perfect for short-season areas.

Peppers, being frost-sensitive, should not be transplanted into the garden until the beginning of June. I suggest growing peppers in five-gallon pots on the deck: containers trap heat, which peppers love.

- ❧ Cool night temperatures will cause blossom drop and prevent fruit from setting. Fruit will develop only when night-time temperatures are consistently warm.

- ❧ Keep your watering consistent. A "drought and soak" cycle will cause the ends of the fruit to go mushy.

- ❧ As a rule, green and red peppers are the same fruit, harvested at different stages of ripening.

Caught Red-handed

THIS IS A CAUTIONARY TALE for all you men out there.

When you have a particularly bountiful crop, you can spend much of August and September storing and preserving vegetables. If you're lucky enough to have a good friend to keep you company, the chore can actually be quite pleasant. But one year we had a harvest my husband Ted will never forget.

Our daughter-in-law Valerie had put a lot of peppers into the trial garden that summer, and her experiments were a bit too successful. We gave peppers away to customers and friends, and still had two huge baskets full of them.

Ted said, "Lois, why don't you chop them up and freeze them? I'll help you."

We turned on the CBC and set to work, chopping and chatting away. I noticed my hands were feeling hot. I thought, "Oh, for heaven's sake, we've got some hot peppers mixed in." I wasn't too

worried, since I was sure that we hadn't picked any really hot peppers like jalapeños and habañeros. Still, my hands were beginning to feel like they were on fire. I asked Ted, "Are your hands hot?"

"No," he shrugged.

We kept chopping and chopping, and from time to time, I'd run to the tap to cool my fingers. I kept asking, "Ted, are you sure your hands aren't hot? Because mine are really getting painful."

"No, no," he said.

Finally, just as we were getting to the end, Ted excused himself. Maybe he should have thought to wash his hands first.

A minute later, I heard his mournful wail from the bathroom: "LO-O-O-ISSSS!" I guess his hands had been hot after all!

He walked very gingerly for the rest of the day. ❧

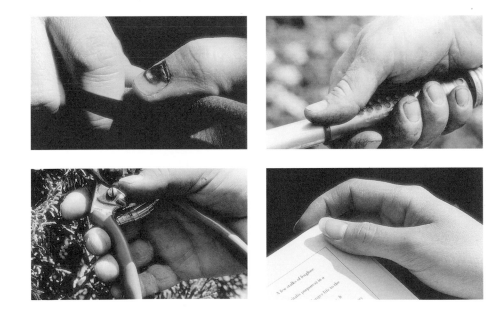

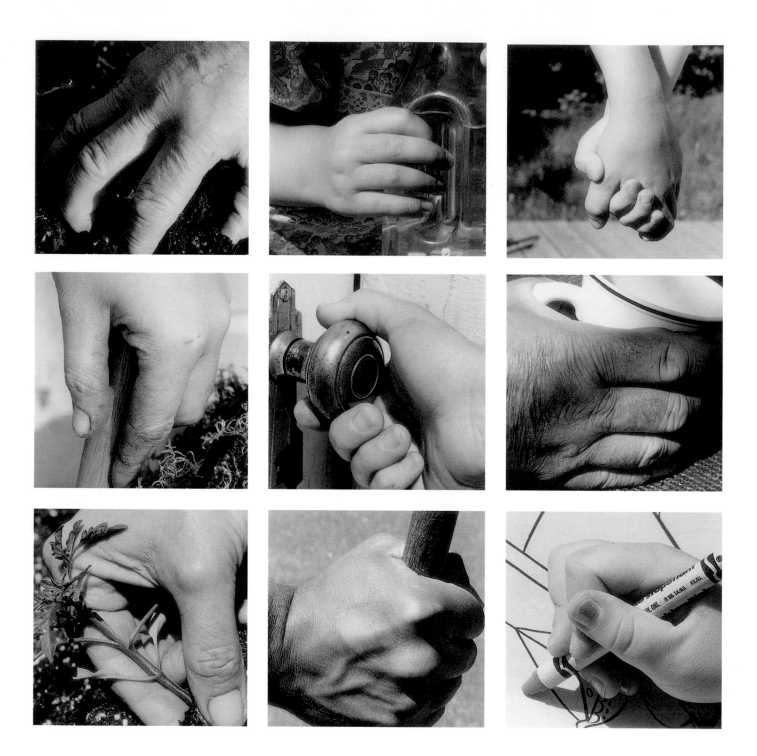

Harvest Season
142

Never Push a Pig

WHEN I WAS FOUR or five years old, I would ride with my Dad down to his stockyards on the outskirts of Buchanan, Saskatchewan. My dad was a stock buyer, and I used to enjoy watching the farmers and stockyard workers loading and unloading the livestock. Although I didn't realize it at the time, my young mind absorbed the whole process in surprising detail.

Many years later, Ted and I tried our hand at raising pigs. I'll always remember when it first came time to take them to market. We needed a chute to get them onto the truck, of course, so Ted set to work building one. I assumed he knew what he was doing, so I didn't pay much attention. However, although he had sound carpentry skills, he had never built a pig chute.

When he brought out the chute. I took one look at it and said, "Ted, you can't use a chute that big for pigs." It was as wide as the half-ton. Pigs need a narrow chute so they can't turn around. Not surprisingly, Ted didn't welcome my unsolicited advice. "What the hell do you know about loading pigs?" he grumbled.

He managed to get three or four pigs part way up the chute. Suddenly, the first pig decided he'd rather be down with his buddies in the pen, so he turned around. Ted blocked his path with a sheet of plywood and let out a whoop, just to show the pig who was boss.

Well, utter chaos ensued. All the pigs were upset now. Every time Ted lunged one way, a pig scrambled another. You might think it's impossible for a pig to climb over the wall of a chute, but get one good and agitated and you'll find out differently. Not a single pig made it all the way onto the truck. Eventually, we threw up our hands and deserted the field of battle.

Ted had to dismantle the chute and rebuild it, while I wisely suppressed the urge to say, "I told you so." When the time came to try again, I suggested, "You should hold a piece of plywood in front of you and walk up the chute behind the pigs." Ted set to work, trying his best, but again the pigs refused to cooperate. Within a minute or two, Ted was yelling and swearing, and the pigs were squealing, grunting, and running around madly.

"Ted, calm down!" I shouted. "You're not going to get anywhere that way!" In his state, that wasn't what he wanted to hear. He continued pushing away at the pigs and sure enough, we didn't get them loaded that day either.

Later in the evening, once Ted and the pigs had settled down, I convinced him to let me give it a try. From what I had seen as a kid, I knew that you had to be very gentle and quiet when loading pigs.

The next day we assembled the pigs for a third attempt. I walked slowly out, crept right up to one of them, put my hand down, and directed a pig up the chute and into the truck, making a gentle "whooshing" sound the whole time. Anytime the pig felt like pausing for a little look around, I'd wait right beside it. When it was ready to continue, off we'd go together.

I herded the pigs into the truck, one by one, while the others patiently, silently waited their turns. Ted could only stand by and chuckle in amazement. From then on, loading the pigs was my job: Ted never could seem to get the knack.

After a few years, it became clear to both of us that we weren't cut out to be pig farmers. And it may be an awful thing to admit, yet those pigs taught me a thing or two about dealing with excitable people. The quiet approach is often the only one that works. If you speak softly and lay a gentle hand on their shoulder, you can lead them almost anywhere. &

Only the Rich...

MY MOTHER-IN-LAW ALWAYS used to say, "Only the rich can afford to buy cheap things." Excellent advice, Grandma Hole. Still, it's often difficult to fight the temptation of buying an item with an enticingly low price tag.

More than once, we learned that lesson the hard way. For years we'd used True Temper stirrup hoes on our farm, after our neighbour Lorna Ross recommended them. They were a little more expensive than other brands, but they lasted for years and were easy to work with. One year, though, another company approached us with their hoes, which were ten dollars cheaper. An offer like that is tough to pass up, so we bought several dozen of them for our field hands.

It didn't take long to figure out that the new hoes were anything but a bargain. The steel was cheap and bent easily, and the sharp blade, crucial for chopping out tough weeds, wore down rapidly.

By the end of each day, there was still plenty of work left undone and everyone was exhausted. After a week or two, the money we'd saved was being eaten up by increased labour costs. We pitched the "bargain" hoes and went back to our old, tried-and-true brand. In fact, some of the stirrup hoes we're using today are 25 to 30 years old.

My sons have learned similar lessons. One fall, Jim was out in the field harvesting cabbage for the supermarkets. Late cabbage has very tough stems, so it can be a brutal job. As Jim was hacking and sawing his way down the row, he noticed that the fellow in the next row was able to slice cleanly through each stem with a single blow.

This man had brought his own knife. It was beautiful, heavy, high-grade steel that stayed sharp even after cutting hundreds of heads. A veteran of many years spent harvesting cabbage, he knew the importance of a strong, sharp knife.

It's worth spending an extra dollar or two on good equipment, and that lesson can be carried through to just about anything you buy. With very few exceptions, you get what you pay for. If you don't spend much, you shouldn't expect much. On the other hand, if you invest a little bit more, chances are you won't regret it.

A customer at the garden centre picked up one of our best shovels one day and expressed polite skepticism about the price tag. "Well," I asked him, "why are you shopping for a shovel?"

"I bent the old one," he replied sheepishly, knowing I had made my point. "Buy this True Temper shovel," I assured him, "and when you get too old to dig, you can pass it on to your grandkids."

Naturally, you should shop around and consider every purchase carefully. If you happen to stumble across an irresistible deal, by all means take advantage of it.

Often, though, the best bargains cost a little bit more. ❧

Let Kids Be Kids

CHILD LABOUR IS A HOT TOPIC these days, as well it should be. All over the world, young people are robbed of their childhoods by unfair and exploitative labour practices. Of course, when Ted and I farmed, we relied an awful lot on kids. If they hadn't helped us so much, we would never have been as successful.

ॐ ॐ ॐ

Work can and should be an integral part of growing up. Children gain a strong sense of satisfaction when they're given the chance to contribute, and they build habits and attitudes that will stick with them long after they've grown up. You just have to find ways to keep the work fun and ensure that it doesn't interfere with other equally important parts of their lives.

When they were young, Bill and Jim were always bringing friends home from school. Their buddies from town loved the chance to be out on a farm. It felt like a different world to them, even though their homes were only a mile or two away.

As the spring evenings lengthened, they'd be up in the field transplanting seedlings. They'd hoe the rows throughout the summer, and they'd help out as the vegetables became ready to harvest.

Sure it was hard work, but the kids wouldn't have kept coming back if they weren't having a good time. It wasn't even the fact that we paid them—although they never complained when I handed out the cheques. When I'd take drinks or popsicles up to them, I felt I was walking into the middle of a rather sweaty social occasion. The radio would be blasting away, competing with a steady stream of jokes and conversation.

I have to admit I pushed them a little bit from time to time. As their energy started to flag, I'd go out there and say, "Come on, kids, just five more minutes!" Ten minutes later, I'd go back out and say, "Just two more minutes!" Somehow though, when the break finally arrived, they always seemed to find the strength to pick up a football and start an impromptu game.

Their parents, naturally, were thrilled at the idea of their children coming out to our place. The kids were happy and healthy, they were earning a few bucks of their own, and if they were tired out at the end of the day, that was a bonus.

I'll never forget one afternoon, though, when a man drove out to the farm, his poor teenage son slumped in the back seat of the car. Something about this man's manner put us off, even before he opened his mouth. He told us, "I want you to put my boy to work. He's a lazy kid, and I want you to show him what real work is like. Straighten him up." The boy had gotten drunk one night, and his father wanted to teach him a lesson. I guess he thought we were running some kind of boot camp.

Ted and I were appalled that this man would think of farm life as punishment. Clearly, he was the one who needed straightening up, not his boy. I don't imagine he ever thought of sitting down to talk with his son, although it was obvious he was very angry at him. I wonder, if we had taken the boy, could we have helped him? But when you're not the parent, when you're only there for a short period of time, there's not much you can do.

If you talk to the kids who worked for us over the years, I don't think you'll hear many complaints. Sure, they'll joke about how we made them slave all day under the hot sun, but they'll also talk about all the good times they had together. Many of them still come out to visit us from time to time, and we're always thrilled to see them.

As a matter of fact, a few of them still work for us. And, if I'm not mistaken, they're still finding a way to have fun on the job. ❧

Society's Loss

MRS. DUROCHER, MY DEAR FRIEND and co-worker, gave me my first strong connection with the native community and my first insights into the difficulties native and Métis people face every day. Every time I saw other people dismiss her, it saddened me to think how much they were missing. Once I got to know Mrs. Durocher, I learned to look at all people more carefully.

When Ted and I first started farming, we truly depended on members of the native community to help us. Unfortunately, we quickly discovered that the problems of alcohol and conflicting cultural values meant we couldn't plan on having their help every day.

Mrs. Durocher's nephew, Peter, was one of the hardest working employees we ever hired. He wasn't always available for work, but Ted made it clear that he was welcome to show up whenever he could, no questions asked.

Peter was a handsome young man, lean and athletic, with a neatly groomed moustache. He was strong, but also shared much of his aunt's grace and agility. I remember when the barn was being shingled, he would slip some nails between his lips and criss-cross the roof like an acrobat, hammering away. The others would struggle to keep up, pausing now and then to watch Peter in amazement. He was quick with a joke and got along well with everybody. Ted often said he breathed a little easier whenever Peter was on the farm.

Then suddenly, one day, Peter was gone. They found him alone in a hotel room, where he had choked to death. He wasn't yet 30.

When you read items like this in the paper, stop and think for a minute. When that person was born, he or she should have the same human potential as your own child. But somewhere, somehow, things went terribly, tragically wrong. I believe very strongly in personal accountability, but it would be foolish and unfair to discount society's role in deaths like these.

I wish I had the answers, but I don't. I try, in my own way, to accept people for what they are and help wherever I can. I just know that we can't afford to simply throw our hands in the air and lament that there's nothing we can do.

Every time our world loses a Peter Durocher, it loses a lot. ❧

The Last Harvest

I'VE BEEN VERY FORTUNATE. We own a successful business. I have my health, a wonderful family, and good friends I can count on. It's a pretty good harvest for a lifetime of work.

I think my success is due to three things: luck, a willingness to learn from the land, and the ability to tackle tough choices. These qualities were crucial at a time of transition that brought fundamental changes to my family and our business.

After finishing their agriculture degrees at the University of Alberta, Bill and Jim each decided they wanted to stay on the farm. That decision meant that Ted and I were going to have to begin sharing control of the business with the boys.

Vegetables had always been the heart of our farm, but by the early 1980s, it became clear that changes were in order. Bill felt there was potential for growth in the greenhouse and garden centre business; Jim agreed. Ted and I were reluctant to admit it, but we knew they were right. We made a major investment to build new greenhouses and started to sell other kinds of plants—bedding plants, roses, trees, and more. We didn't get rid of the vegetables right away, but their disappearance was gradually becoming inevitable.

The retail vegetable business was winding down, but Bill wanted to expand our wholesale carrot production. Our Nantes carrots were of far better quality than those sold in grocery stores, and he thought we could break into the market. It wasn't easy, but we put our hearts into it. We worked hard and learned the new business, and after a few years, we gained over 50 percent of the fresh carrot market in both Edmonton and Calgary.

But now we were running two businesses: a wholesale vegetable operation and a retail garden centre. Common sense tells us that businesses fail because they don't find enough success, but too much success can be equally dangerous. Both operations were prospering, but our efforts were divided. It was only a matter of time before one or the other would begin to suffer. We had to make a choice: concentrate on one business or watch them both slowly deteriorate. In 1991, after weeks of discussion around the kitchen table, we agreed to get out of carrots. The next harvest would be our last.

Bill and Jim were tremendously proud of what they'd help to create and wanted to wrap up the carrot business with a perfect harvest. It looked as if Mother Nature was going to cooperate, delivering exceptional weather. The season was long, hot, and sunny, with just the right amount of rain. It didn't last.

We had about an acre of carrots left to harvest when the weather suddenly turned bad. Sleet poured down, smashing the leafy carrot tops into the mud. While Jim drove the tractor, Bill stood on the harvester with a hockey stick, flipping away the wet, soggy greens to keep them from jamming the machine. It was a long, slow, wet job. I told them that letting an acre or so lie in the field wasn't the end of the world, but they had to harvest every last carrot. They needed that sense of closure.

So they slogged on, harvesting foot by laborious foot, swearing a blue streak every time the harvester jammed. Despite the odds, they actually managed to get every last carrot out of the muck. Judging by the smiles on their faces, I don't think they could have been more pleased if they'd dug up a crop of gold nuggets.

By the time we shipped the last batch, we'd sold over two million pounds of carrots: our last crop was our largest and most profitable ever. Ted wanted something to remember the business by, so he snatched up the very last bag from the packing line. It contained the last of six million pounds of carrots grown and packed on our farm. We ate those last carrots with mingled pride and sadness, and when we had finished, Ted framed the bag. It remains on the wall next to his desk to this day.

ॐॐॐ

I felt mixed emotions as I watched the big eighteen-wheeler take away that last shipment. There was a twinge of sadness, but I knew that the boys would turn the greenhouse and garden centre into something special. I was so proud of all they'd done, of everything they'd learned. It brought back a powerful memory of that first visit to the farm, when Ted smelled the earth and told me how rich it was. How right he'd been.

Although we're not selling vegetables anymore, the land continues to sustain me and my family. Valerie and I still tend our original vegetable garden, and I get great joy from sharing fresh produce with family and friends. This land has given us so much—health, prosperity, and a thousand priceless lessons. But the most important thing I learned from our farm is simply that there's still so much more to learn. That lesson, I think, is the true harvest. ✑

...a savoury challenge...

Celery

THIS FUSSY VEGETABLE was one of the first to go when we phased out market gardening, because we simply couldn't support its growth requirements in our climate. Bill remembers hating celery because its almost unquenchable thirst required so many trips down to the river to start the irrigation pump.

We once trucked a whole load of celery to a major buyer, who turned it down. The vegetables were perfectly edible, but heavy rains had splattered dirt in the inner portions of the plant, where it's impossible to clean until the stalks are broken up. For a home gardener, this isn't a problem: the celery can be washed as it is eaten. But for us, with thousands of plants to store and sell, it was a major problem. Water and soil, two crucial elements to celery's success, can also pose the plant's greatest challenges.

Stalk of Choice: Utah 52-70

This is the old standby, an early-maturing celery that can't be beat for flavour and texture.

I grow my celery from seed, using indoor seedling containers. Once the seedlings have two true leaves—about the end of May—transplant them to the garden. A 3 m row (about 20 plants) is enough to provide a dozen meals, plus numerous snacks, for a family of 4.

Celery isn't the easiest plant to grow. For one thing, it needs a long growing season; for another, it demands a lot of fertilizer and water. Yet it can't tolerate heavy rain, because rain splashes dirt onto the plants, and dirt carries with it soil-borne bacteria to which celery is vulnerable.

Use the whole thing

The great thing about celery is that you can eat the whole vegetable. My daughter-in-law Valerie sprinkles celery seed over salads or adds it to soup. I like to use the leaves in soup and to make stock. Because of the climate, our celery tends to be deeper green and have a stronger flavour. It's not the best for eating raw, but it makes superb soups and stews, and adds terrific flavour to any recipe that requires cooked celery.

Celeriac

Celeriac, a ugly relative of celery, has never been the world's most popular vegetable. I only discovered the joys of this vegetable when a wise old German lady urged me to try it. I can tell you, after giving celeriac a fair hearing in the kitchen, I fell in love with it. It's just beautiful. As they say, you can't judge a book by its cover.

I transplant celeriac outdoors from the middle to the end of May, once the seedlings have two true leaves. I normally put in at least a dozen plants. Celeriac is pretty easy to grow; to ensure a good crop, keep weeds under control and provide a consistent supply of water and fertilizer.

❧ Celery leaves contain high concentrations of psoralens, chemicals that can weaken skin's resistance to ultraviolet radiation. If you're going to be working with celery on a bright day, wear sunscreen or a pair of gloves to avoid sunburn.

❧ Celery is supposed to be the selinon mentioned in Homer's *Odyssey*.

...best in poor soil...
Rutabagas

RUTABAGAS ARE commonly confused with turnips, and no wonder: rutabagas have purple tops and yellowish brown bottoms, while turnips have purple tops and white bottoms. But rutabagas are also larger, sweeter, and later-maturing than turnips.

The first time we grew rutabagas (also known as Swede turnips), Ted spread manure on the field to fertilize it. When harvest time came, we discovered the rutabagas were covered with hair and tasted terrible. There was also excessive growth and splitting. This was how we discovered that root crops should never be spread with manure unless it's well rotted. We later learned, to our amazement, that rutabagas actually grow better in poor soil. In rich soil, rutabagas grow so rapidly that they often split, leading to disease and rot. Sandy or heavy clay soils, without a lot of nitrogen, produce the best results: the plants enjoy slow but steady growth and turn out large and smooth.

Jim remembers eating rutabagas raw for a quick pick-me-up while harvesting. Its crunchy flesh is cool and refreshing, a perfect snack in the field!

* Don't worry about fall frosts hurting your rutabaga crop: their flavour actually improves after a hard frost!

* Most rutabagas are "hot-waxed" by commercial growers to prevent moisture loss during shipping and storage. This is simply a thin layer of paraffin that will come off with the skin when you peel the rutabaga.

* More than any other vegetable, the rutabaga's close relative the turnip needs the right kind of soil. To avoid huge, ugly top growth, turnips should be planted in poor, not rich, soil. Planting in a sandy soil works well: the roots are easier to work with and cleaner when pulled.

Root of Choice: Laurentian
The Laurentian is the most popular rutabaga grown today, notable for its deep-purple top and creamy yellow flesh. It has a smooth texture and a mild, pleasant taste; it doesn't get woody or pithy.

If you sow as soon as the ground can be worked, the roots will be ready for harvest in late summer; if you prefer a fall crop, seed in the first week of June. One large plant provides about three servings of rutabaga.

…weird but delicious…

Kohlrabi

Ask anyone in the know what the weirdest vegetable in the garden is and they'll probably answer, "Kohlrabi." If you've never seen this unique vegetable, picture a smooth red or green ball with long, thin shoots topped with bushy leaves growing up from the ball's sides. It's the closest thing to an alien vegetable that I've ever seen!

A tough customer

Harvesting kohlrabi probably requires more brute force than any other vegetable. We chop off the roots with a hatchet: the stems are very durable and won't let go without a fight. When I grow kohlrabi, I harvest it when it's about the size of a tennis ball—this is the "gourmet" size. You can let them get larger, but you'll need to remove the portions that have grown tough and fibrous.

Root of Choice: Granlibakken

It's been a while, but at last we have a new variety of kohlrabi. Granlibakken is very tender and has a fantastic sweet flavour. Great both raw and cooked, Granlibakken bulbs resist getting tough and woody.

I seed kohlrabi in April, but you can do it as late as June if you'd like a later harvest. A 1 m row will yield about 15 globes, enough to make several suppers for a family of 4.

Kohlrabi is a resilient plant, perfect for children's gardens. But be sure to help the kids with the harvesting!

Try something new

If you haven't tried kohlrabi before, you're in for a treat! Grow a small number of plants and experiment. Green varieties mature early; purple varieties mature somewhat later. If you're already a fan of kohlrabi, try small, successive plantings, to give you fresh produce throughout the season. I always like to give a few globes away, to introduce more people to this unusual vegetable.

Remove the tough outer layer and inside you'll find a delightfully versatile vegetable. Serve it raw on a vegetable platter, toss it into a stir-fry, or add it to soups and stews for richer flavour. Kohlrabi also makes a great lunch-box addition or a light mid-afternoon snack.

❧ The word kohlrabi derives from the Latin word *caulorapa,* which reflects the plant's origins: *caulo* means "cabbage," *rapa* means "turnip."

Afterword
The End of an Era

IN THE EARLY 1980s, Ted and I faced a difficult decision. Our old red barn, which had been the focal point of our business for decades, was really showing its age. Yet tearing it down seemed unthinkable. The barn held a strong emotional attachment, not only for our family but for people from miles around.

One of the local old-timers remembered seeing the barn when he arrived in 1903, and it had been around long before that. It was certainly the first thing that caught Ted's eye when he found the property all those years ago, and it was one of my indelible memories from our first visit to the farm together. When we began market gardening, our newspaper ads read, "Come on out to the old red barn!" It wasn't just another old farm building, it was a much-loved landmark. The bright-red barn with its big white letters had become a local personality.

For years we had been postponing the inevitable, patching cracked and broken planks one by one until the entire floor was as rough as a country road. Although our customers and staff knew to watch their step, people still managed to trip almost every day. Fortunately, we never had any serious accidents.

Then, one morning, Dave Grice and Bill were moving loads of vegetables from the bottom of the barn to the tables above. As usual, the boys were pushing their wheelbarrows very carefully: if the load tipped, all the vegetables had to be taken outside and washed again.

All of a sudden, one of Dave's feet plunged straight through the floor. Everyone rushed over to make sure he was okay. Dave hauled his leg out of the hole, laughing, and proudly pointed out that he hadn't spilled a single carrot.

Even before the laughter died down, the implications started to sink in. If one person had broken through the floor, it was only a matter of time before it happened again. Next time, maybe it wouldn't be a laughing matter.

At first, we looked into restoring the barn from the ground up. We hired a backhoe operator to dig down next to an exterior wall, to allow us to inspect the foundation. The moment he removed the dirt, the entire wall shifted two feet. Whoever had built the barn originally had planted untreated timbers directly into the soil. Over time, the entire foundation had rotted away.

We realized we had no choice. One sad morning, family and staff lined up for one last photograph in front of the still-bright red barn.

We talked quietly together as we watched the Caterpillar driver set to work. The barn was so important to so much of what we had been and done. We remembered the squawking chickens that used to be housed in the barn. We recalled those endless winter days cutting seed potatoes. I thought back to the first day we moved our vegetable sales into the barn, all clean and freshly white-washed. Valerie remembered when Ted had hung a huge Commonwealth flag from the roof during the Games in 1978. Then everyone tensed as the Caterpillar moved in.

The driver knew what he was doing. He wanted the barn to fall away from the road, so he first carefully knocked out the supporting timbers in two of the corners. Miraculously, the barn remained standing. Then he slowly approached the front wall and gave it a gentle push with the blade. The building shuddered for an instant, then collapsed wearily in a billowing cloud of dust. I looked over at Ted. He had silently turned his back on the scene, unable to watch.

When the barn came down, it literally felt like a death. Even though it was expected, the final moment still came as a terrible shock. Some of the staff members were openly weeping. Even Dave, who had complained about the barn for years, said he felt as if he'd been punched in the stomach.

A chapter in our lives closed that morning. With the barn gone, we were leaving behind a comfortable past and heading towards an exciting but uncertain future.

More than fourteen years have passed since then, and our business has multiplied several times in size. Still, almost every day we get a customer who says, "You know, I've been coming out here since the days of the old red barn." They sound as if they're talking about a wonderful friend, someone long departed and deeply missed.

We know how they feel.

About the Photography

WHEN WE BEGAN shooting for this book, we set out to create visual representations of events and places that existed only in the mind. The old barn was gone, the people and situations had changed. Thus in order to capture the essence of Lois' stories, we had to move beyond the literal.

We began with a few core concepts: that the images would present a different angle on the subject; that they would be evocative rather than representational; and that they would do more than just support the text. Using alternative processes, we attempted to transform the photographs into works of art in their own right. As a result, most of the images in this book were created with photographic techniques, very few were manipulated on the computer.

Many of the images were shot in black and white, allowing more freedom to play with light and shadow and permitting the reader to focus on the composition, undistracted by colour. Some were shot with infrared film and others with an extremely fast film to push the grain and add texture.

The colour images presented a bigger challenge. We worked with the physical angle of the camera and played with film and processing to create different emotions. Many times we used multiple shots to create one image, allowing us to expand the image beyond the limits of the film's boundaries.

Some of the more interesting techniques used were polaroid transfers, which involved transferring polaroid images to handmade paper; cross-processing, which increased contrast and created saturated colours; and painting with light, which allowed us to add light in specific areas. By shooting many of the vegetables on a light table, we were able to capture their luminescence.

It was our intention to create a book whose images are as rich and varied as the stories they accompany. We hope you enjoy it.

Akemi Matusbuchi & Bruce Keith

Images in this book were taken primarily with a Nikon F-3 using a Tamron Macro f2.8 lens, using Fuji Provia 100. In addition, a Hasselblad 500 CM medium format camera and a 4x5 Sinar were also used.

HOLE'S

૭૪૭૪૭૪

Art Direction	BRUCE TIMOTHY KEITH
Editorial	LESLIE VERMEER
Writing & Research	SCOTT ROLLANS, EARL J. WOODS
Principal Photography	AKEMI MATSUBUCHI
Additional Photography	IAN GRANT INC.